PAUL ELLIS

KINGSPRESS
Birkenhead, New Zealand

The Gospel in Twenty Questions

ISBN: 978-1-927230-10-7
Copyright © 2013 by Paul Ellis

Dedication: This is for everyone asking good questions.

ENDORSEMENTS

"Paul Ellis's new book is an absolute must read. It is packed full of godly wisdom and powerful truths that will thrill and excite you. Paul takes deep theological concepts and makes them simple and easy for anyone to grasp. This is one of the best books I have ever read since becoming a believer over thirty years ago. I will be encouraging every believer I know to get this book and absorb what the Holy Spirit has revealed to Paul in its pages."

— ED ELLIOTT
   aka "The Vagabond Evangelist"

"When I stumbled upon the beautiful revelation of the new covenant, it was Paul Ellis's writing that affirmed and helped me make sense of my newfound freedom. Now, in one brilliant book, Paul has answered the biggest questions people have about the gospel of grace. This book is for everyone who has a sneaking suspicion that a life of religious duty might not be what Christ intended — that just maybe, he offers something more."

— ERIC DYKSTRA
   pastor, The Crossing Church, USA
   author of *Grace on Tap*

"Dr. Paul Ellis has hit another home run with his new book! In it Paul answers complex questions with clarity and simplicity. This book, along with his first, will serve well as a basic handbook for discipleship. The gospel is liberating!"

— PAUL C. MATA
   senior pastor, Word for All Nations, Philippines

"Too often we ask the wrong questions and this leads to wrong understanding. Paul Ellis helps us ask the right questions and better still, draw the right conclusions. This book will inspire you as you think through those deep-seated questions that are within every human soul. It will ensure that your thoughts not only end at the right place but start there as well."

— CLINT BYARS
   founder of Forward Ministries
   author of *Good God*

"Paul Ellis's second book answers questions that many believers are asking today. This is a great book for believers transitioning from the old covenant to the new. This is a much-needed book for the grace revolution sweeping Christendom."

— ROBBIE TAN
pastor, Grace Generation Church, New Zealand

"This book sheds light on both easy and tough questions while at the same time drawing you deeper into the love, grace and wonder that is the gospel of Christ. Well written, easy to read and bursting with divine goodness!"

— CORNEL MARAIS
founder of CharismaMinistries.org
author of *So You Think Your Mind is Renewed?*

"I'm such a huge fan of questions and this book has many of the important questions everyone should ask. Easy to understand, and overflowing with God's grace, *The Gospel in Twenty Questions* is sure to help many find freedom from struggle and strife."

— D. R. SILVA
author of *It's All About Jesus: What They Never Told You in Church*

"A life of faith is one that questions everything. It's a kind of life that's not afraid to ask 'Why?' If you're the kind of person who isn't afraid of questions then you'll enjoy reading this book. As with all Paul's writing, it's well worth the read."

— MICK MOONEY
author of *SNAP: Everyone Has A Breaking Point*

"More than ever before, the gospel must be proclaimed with both courage and clarity; courage to a culture consumed with complacency, and clarity to a church confused by inconsistency. It is for these reasons and more, that I gladly commend Paul Ellis to you."

— CHAD M. MANSBRIDGE
senior pastor, Bayside Church International, Australia
author of *He Qualifies You*

Contents

Preface: Ask and You Shall Receive

"Every revolution starts with a question." ~D.R. Silva

Questions are keys. They open doors and unlock treasures. Questions are stepping stones to revelation and doorways to discovery.

A good question can take you places. It can free you from unhealthy mindsets and set you on the path to wholeness and abundant living. A good question can change your life.

We are born asking questions. We grow up asking questions. When we stop asking, we stop growing.

As a pastor, I helped people wrestle with the questions of life. Who am I? What should I do? Where should I go? Who should I marry? Your success in life is determined by how well you answer these sorts of questions.

As a university professor, I taught that science is about asking good questions. Ask a good question and new discoveries will surely follow. But the wrong question will never lead you to the right answer.

Asking questions is healthy. We are defined by the questions we ask, and our search for answers is what makes us who we are.

God made us curious because ultimately all questions lead to him. How tragic, then, that religion tends to discourage questions. A famous preacher once said, "Good Christians, like slaves and soldiers, ask no questions." In other words, "Do what you're told and don't make trouble." Others dismiss questions as a sign of faithlessness. "Who are you to question God? Just believe."

Religion stifles questions, but Jesus encouraged them. "Ask and you shall receive" (John 16:24). Asking is how we receive. If your life lacks direction and answers it's probably because you haven't asked the right questions.

Jesus said we come to the kingdom of God like children. Children ask questions all the time. I am often amazed by my children's questions and I delight in responding to them. So does your heavenly Father. The insecure may be threatened by your questions, but he is not. Like the good Father he is, he welcomes them, for he knows your questions will lead you towards a deeper revelation of his love.

1

The freedom to ask questions without fear is a hallmark of a healthy relationship. But if our questions are to be of value, they must eventually lead to answers.

For years I believed, "Jesus is the answer," but I didn't know the question. Or rather, I thought Jesus was the answer to a very limited question—namely, how can I be saved? That's a fine question and an important one. But Jesus is the answer to much more than that. The gospel of grace declares Jesus is the answer to every need you will ever have.

I was a Christian for 30 years before I realized this. I used to think *I* was the answer. Success in life was all about me and how hard I worked and how well I followed Christian principles. Then one day the grace of God came in like a flood and washed away the sandcastle of my DIY religion.

Most of us are familiar with religion in one form or another. Religion is simply the universal quest for self-improvement.

Grace is different. Grace isn't a bunch of rules for you to keep. And grace is not God's lubricant for greasing the cogs of self effort. Grace is a Person living his life through you. Living under grace is like being married, only more so. It's the adventure of life shared with Christ.

When I first heard the gospel of grace, I had many questions. One of my first questions was concerning the church at Laodicea. "If we're kept by grace alone, why does Jesus threaten to vomit out those who are lukewarm?" Nobody could tell me. So I did what I do when faced with a hard question: I began to write. I asked the Holy Spirit for help and he gave me revelation. He showed me how to read the Bible through the lens of grace.

There's no point in writing if no one's reading so I started posting my half-baked answers on a blog called Escape to Reality. To my surprise, readers responded with questions of their own. Hundreds of them. The blog became a lightning rod for questions people were too afraid or too shy to ask.

It wasn't long before readers started saying, "You should write a book." So I did, and *The Gospel in Ten Words* was published in 2012. That book answers questions like, "Who am I?" and "Why am I here?" It's a book full of stories. But while that book will give you a good grasp of your identity in Christ, it leaves unasked many questions about God and his gospel. Hence the book you are now reading.

The Gospel in Twenty Questions is the book I was looking for when I first came to grace. This book is an attempt to deal with the questions I regularly hear from E2R readers.

You will notice this book is not entitled, *The Gospel in Twenty Answers*. I don't claim to have all the answers but I do hope you like my questions. To paraphrase Voltaire, judge me by my questions rather than my answers.[1]

Despite the title, there are more than 200 questions in this book. There are questions about God, grace, sin, forgiveness, the Holy Spirit, communion, healing, freedom, faith, unbelief, eternal security, heavenly treasures, and numerous "tough" scriptures. There's even a question about the Laodiceans.

This isn't the sort of book you need to read from cover to cover, so let me suggest two ways to read it. You can dip into those chapters that interest you, or you can launch out from the scripture index found at the back of the book. However you approach it, I hope you will begin your journey by asking the most important question of all.

This is the question I ask in chapter 1 …

1. Who's Your Daddy?

When my first child was born, there were some complications and she had to spend a few days in a special care ward. During that time, she was kept in an incubator and the only way I could touch her was by putting my arms through holes in the side of the incubator wall. She was only a few hours old when I came to her, stroked her, and asked her a question.

"Who's your daddy?"

I didn't expect her to answer, so I answered for her.

"I'm your daddy, and I love you."

It thrilled me to tell her this again and again.

"Who's your daddy? I am. It's me. I'm that guy. I'm your father, you're my baby, and I love you."

The communication was all one-way but that was fine with me. I couldn't shut up. I had just become a father, and my heart was fit to burst. This little girl belonged to me and I belonged to her. There were many things I wanted to tell her, but the first and most important thing she needed to hear was that I was her daddy and I loved her.

She's older now, but I have never stopped telling her that I'm her daddy and I never will. My desire is that she will live her entire life knowing who I am and how much I love her.

What is the most important question?

The most important question you will ever ask is, "Who is my father?" Your answer to this question will influence every other question of life. Who am I? Where did I come from? Why am I here?

Get the father question wrong and you will miss it on every other issue. Your identity will be muddled, and you will have no lasting security. In your legitimate desire to define yourself, you may settle for inferior choices such as career or ministry. "I am a doctor." "I am a pastor." But the truth is you are more than what you do. You are your father's child.

But who is your father?

My wife, Camilla, and I recently had lunch with a primary school teacher. This lady told us her school had just started a breakfast club for poor kids. The purpose of the breakfast club is to provide toast, milk, and cereal for students who come to school with empty stomachs. Although we live in one of the world's wealthiest nations, in our city, many thousands of kids don't have enough to eat. The breakfast clubs are a great idea because learning is hard when you're hungry.

"What kind of families do these breakfast kids come from?" I asked.

"Teenage mothers with no parenting skills," was her quick reply. "The fathers are long gone, and many of the moms have boyfriends who view these children as nuisances. It's not uncommon for the boyfriends to beat the kids."

My heart breaks for these children. I wonder how they will turn out given that the dominant male influence in their lives comes from men who don't love them. I wonder what kind of fathers the boys will become, since they have no fathers of their own. And I wonder if my children will be providing breakfast clubs for *their* children.

The worst part is that this story is hardly unusual. The kids in the breakfast club are merely the latest victims in an ancient cycle of poor parenting. Our family tree dates back to Adam, who fathered a murderer. Is it any exaggeration to say that the number one problem in this world is fatherlessness? Pick any wife-beater, drug dealer, or pedophile, and the odds are good you will find someone who had a bad dad. Fathers matter.

I know something about fatherlessness because my own dad died when I was eight years old. As a boy growing up with no father, the odds were stacked against me. Only they weren't. By the grace of God, I was delivered from Adam's cursed family and adopted into another. I knew who my Father was and how much he loved me, and that has made all the difference.

Jesus answers the most important question: "Who's your Father? God is your Father!"

In the Old Testament, no one dared speak of the Almighty in such familiar terms. God was the Creator, the Lord of heaven and earth. He was a distant mystery glimpsed occasionally by the prophets and select others. Back then, people prayed formal and lofty prayers to the God of Abraham, Isaac, and Jacob. Then Jesus came and said we should pray like this:

Our Father in heaven ... (Matthew 6:9)

Can you imagine the shock of those who heard these words? "God is my *Father*? Are you sure about that, Jesus? Surely you mean he's *your* father, not mine." Yet in his Sermon on the Mount Jesus identifies God as *your* Father and *our* Father no less than sixteen times. This was good news then and it's good news now. The One who measures the universe in his hand is *your Daddy*.

What is God's name?

Before Jesus, no one called God "Father." It just wasn't done. But after Jesus, every New Testament writer spoke this way. James declared, "Every good and perfect gift comes down from the Father." John boasted, "How great is the Father's love." And Paul began nearly all of his letters with, "Grace and peace to you from God our Father."[1]

The saints of the Old Testament had many names for God, but Jesus gave us the best name of all: "*Abba*, Father" (Mark 14:36). *Abba* is not the name of a distant and mysterious God. *Abba* is your heavenly Father who cares for you and longs for you to know him. *Abba* is your Daddy who loves you so much he sent his Son to tell you.

Why did Jesus come? Jesus came to reveal God the Father to you. He came so that you might know who you truly are. He came that you might experience the abundant life of living as the apple of your Father's eye.

Why did I write this book? I wrote it so that you might know your heavenly Father is the very definition of awesome. He's better and bigger than you think he is. And I wrote it so that you might know you are his beloved child.

Your heavenly Father is for you. He has tilted the universe in your favor. With a Father like this, how can you fail?

Jesus said, "Father, glorify your name!" (John 12:28). What is the name of God that Jesus wants to glorify? He just told us. It's Father. He has other names, but this is the name he wants us to use when we talk to him.

My purpose in this book is Jesus' purpose. It's to draw your attention to a God named Father. This is the name Jesus gave us and it is the name we esteem above all others. You need to see God as Jesus did — as a Father.

"But Paul, you're talking about the Ancient of Days and the Most High God." I am, and he is all those things and infinitely more besides. He is magnificent beyond words and beautiful beyond comprehension. But above all titles and all names, he is your Father and my Father. This book is not a Bible-study; it's a Daddy-study.

Theologians like to ask, "What was Jesus' favorite subject?" Some observe that he spoke often about the kingdom. Others note that he spoke much about money and love. But Jesus' favorite subject by a long stretch was his Father. Everything he said and everything he did was grounded in the relationship he shared with his Father.

"I do what I see my Father doing," said Jesus. "I speak what I hear him speaking."[2] Near the end of his life, Jesus prayed,

> Righteous Father, though the world does not know you, I know you, and they know that you have sent me. I have made you known to them, and will continue to make you known... (John 17:25–26)

Jesus is in the business of making the Father known. Yet many don't know God as their Father. Like the saints of old, they may see him as Lord but not *Abba*. It's as if Jesus never came.

What is God like?

A.W. Tozer once said, "What comes into our minds when we think about God is the most important thing about us."[3] Your picture of God is the single greatest influence on your life. Define God and you define yourself. For instance, if you imagine God as a terrifying punisher, you'll likely be fearful and guilt-ridden. If you see him as a semi-deaf sky-Santa, you'll likely be a superstitious worrier. And if you believe him to be distant or dead, chances are you'll act as a little god of your own little world. How you see him affects how you see yourself.

Your view of God matters, but what is God really like?

Read the prophetic visions in the Bible and you will discover some truly fantastic images. Isaiah saw the Lord wearing a colossal robe and surrounded by six-winged singing angels. Ezekiel saw God as a glowing metal man wrapped in a rainbow. And Daniel saw a white-haired ageless figure seated on a burning throne with burning wheels. But these prophetic pictures are only glimpses into God's nature. They describe aspects but not the whole picture. If you want to know what God is really like, you need to look elsewhere.[4]

> In the past God spoke to our ancestors through the prophets at many times and in various ways, but in these last days he has spoken to us by his Son ... The Son is the radiance of God's glory and the exact representation of his being ... (Hebrews 1:1–3a)

What is the Father like? He is exactly like the Son. Or the Son is exactly like the Father. God is like Jesus. Not roughly so, but exactly so. Jesus said, "Anyone who has seen me has seen the Father" (John 14:9). If you ran into God the Father at a party you might mistake him for Jesus or vice versa. That's how similar they are.

This similarity makes it easy for us to dismiss the silly caricatures of manmade religion. Since Jesus is not a semi-deaf sky-Santa, then neither is God. And since Jesus is not a terrifying punisher, neither is God. Your heavenly Father is exactly like Jesus.

Maybe you think God is a bookkeeper recording all your sins. Perhaps someone told you, "When you get to heaven, they will play a video of your life and all your secret sins will be exposed." But God is not like that. How do we know? Because Jesus is not like that. Jesus didn't shame sinners. He loved them and had dinner with them and introduced them to his Father.

9

Or maybe you think God is a passive and ineffectual sovereign who lets the universe run on auto-pilot. "Everything that happens is his will. If I get sick, God ordained it. If my baby dies, it's because God took him home." But God is not like that. How do we know? Because Jesus is not like that. Jesus is not a fatalist. His desire was to see the Father's will done on earth as it is in heaven. This is why he healed the sick and raised the dead.

Or maybe you think your sins put you in danger of an angry God. "God hates sinners and plans to crush them under his feet without mercy." But God is not like that. How do we know? Because Jesus is not like that. Jesus is a friend of sinners; therefore, God is a friend of sinners too. Indeed, he is the best friend a sinner could have.

God the Father and God the Son don't have separate agendas. God is not in heaven recording your sins while Jesus is forgiving them. Nor is he giving you sicknesses so Jesus can heal you. The Father and the Son are exactly alike, they're on the same page, and they have the same heart. Jesus said, "I and the Father are one" (John 10:30).

What about the God of the Old Testament?

Some find it difficult to reconcile the Jesus of the Gospels with the stern God they've been raised with. "Jesus I like, but I'm not too sure about his Dad." They picture Jesus as a big brother sheltering them from the blows of an angry and abusive Father. But God is not like that at all. How do we know? Because Jesus is not like that, and Jesus is the exact representation of the Father.

"But didn't Moses say God would curse us if we broke his laws?" Moses may have said it, but Jesus never did. Moses had good reasons for saying what he did when he did, and we'll get to those later, but Moses had only a partial understanding of God's true character. Jesus is the complete picture. Moses had a glimpse, but Jesus gives us the full 360-degree panorama.

I am sometimes asked, "How does the angry God of the Old Testament fit with the nice God of the New?" This question makes it sound like there is more than one God or that God has changed over time. Perhaps he went to anger management classes. But the truth is God never changes. God has always been our loving Father. The first man, Adam, was called a son of God (Luke 3:38). The problem is not that God stopped being our Father. The problem is we ran away from home.

The so-called "God of the Old Testament" is a fuzzy photograph taken with a telephoto lens by those who could not appreciate what they were looking at. Moses, Elijah, and the other Old Testament prophets had a revelation of God but they did not fully know him. Before Jesus, nobody did. God is simply too big for mortal minds to grasp.

> No one has ever seen God, but the one and only Son, who is himself God and is in closest relationship with the Father, has made him known. (John 1:18)

The only person who can accurately explain God is God himself, and he did this by sending us his Son. Jesus is God explaining himself to the human race. Jesus is the answer to the question, "What is God like?"

What kind of God does Jesus reveal?

> For God so loved the world that he gave his one and only Son ... God did not send his Son into the world to condemn the world, but to save the world through him. (John 3:16–17)

Jesus reveals a loving God who cares deeply for us and will not let us slip quietly into the night of our sin. Our forefather Adam rejected God in the Garden, but our heavenly Father did not reject us. We built a wall, but he made a door. We ran and hid, but he came and found us.

God sent Jesus because he wants us to know how much he loves us. He's not interested in condemning us or treating us as our sins deserve. His desire is to rescue every last one of us, from the best of us to the worst of us. His Father-heart beats for more children. It beats for you and for your family. It beats for your neighbors and those kids at the breakfast club. It even beats for their dead-beat dads and their negligent mothers. The Father's heart of love beats for the whole world.

"Paul, that sounds like you're preaching unconditional love." Is there any other kind? For too long religion has prostituted the love of God by telling us we must do stuff before our Father will love us. This is the greatest crime ever inflicted on the human race. It has left us orphaned, messed up, and in the pigpen of dead works. Manmade religion says God is angry and must be appeased. But Jesus shows us that God's face is shining on us with love and grace.

> We have seen his glory, the glory of the one and only Son, who came from the Father, full of grace and truth ... For the law was given through Moses; grace and truth came through Jesus Christ. (John 1:14b, 17)

If the law came through Moses and grace came through Jesus Christ, then God the Father must be a grace-giver, not a law-giver. And since the Son came full of grace and truth, the Father must be full of grace and truth too. And he is. He sits on a throne of grace, not a throne of law.

Some imagine that God gives us law while Jesus gives us grace. God hammers us with holy judgments while Jesus gives us cuddles. This is nuts. It'll lead you to cling to the Son but run from the Father.

The good news declares that Jesus is the embodiment of the Father's grace. Jesus is fantastically gracious, but he is no more gracious than God himself. They are the dynamic duo of graciousness. There is no attempt to manipulate you into cooperation. There is just grace upon grace radiating from the throne of grace.

Life is full of cares and worries, but Jesus said, "Do not worry, for your heavenly Father knows your needs" (see Matthew 6:31–32). And Jesus wasn't talking about great spiritual needs, but ordinary, everyday needs like food and clothing. The bad news of the orphaned life says, "You are on your own and nobody cares." But the good news Jesus proclaimed says, "You are not alone and your heavenly Father cares about even the smallest details of your life."

Perhaps you have come to this book with some questions. Who am I? Why am I here? Is God angry with me? Good fathers love it when their kids ask questions, but you will never get good answers unless you see God as your good Father.

Who am I? You are your Father's dearly loved child.

Why am I here? Because your Father loved you into existence. You are his dream come true.

Is God mad at me? Nope. He rejoices over you with singing.

Can he forgive me for the things I've done? He already did.

Does he love me for who I am? He thinks you're great! You're a one-of-a-kind special and he delights in you.

Will he disown me if I sin? Never. Would you disown your own children?

What does he expect from me? He expects you to settle in his love and flourish in his grace.

Life is more than eating and drinking and paying bills. The abundant life that comes through Jesus is nothing less than the adventure of exploring the limitless love of a great God. It's riding atop the shoulders of the One who made all things.

Whether you are in the pigpen of dead works or the special care ward for broken people, you need to know that your heavenly Father loves you like crazy. He reaches down with love in his eyes and healing in his hands and asks, "Who's your Daddy? *I'm* your Daddy, you're my child, and I love you."

This is the good news an orphaned world most needs to hear.

2. What Really Happened at the Cross?

In the movie *Taken*, Liam Neeson plays a man called Bryan whose daughter has been abducted by a human trafficking ring. The outlook is not good. The daughter is bound for slavery and her father is far away. But Bryan speaks to the trafficker on the phone and delivers one of the best movie quotes of recent times:

> If you let my daughter go now, that'll be the end of it. I will not look for you, I will not pursue you. But if you don't, I will look for you, I will find you, and I will kill you.[1]

This line resonates because it speaks to the grizzly-bear heart of every father. "You touch my kids, and I will come for you." This is what dads do. We protect our children from wicked men like that slaver. And if our children do get taken, we come for them with everything we have.

This is exactly how it is with our heavenly Father. In Genesis chapter 2 God gave us life and liberty, but in Genesis chapter 3 we allowed ourselves to be taken in by the lies of a slaver and lost it all. The consequences were terrible and we're still paying the price. But in the dark hour of our Fall, our loving Father declared war on our abductor. He looked the serpent in the eye and spoke of One who would come and visit Neeson-like vengeance on his head.

And on the cross, God delivered on his promise.

Why did Jesus come and die?

Since the Fall, mankind has viewed God through a cracked lens. We have projected our brokenness onto a God we do not know and created a deity in our fallen likeness. This manmade god embodies our deepest fears and insecurities. He is the law incarnate who counts our sins and grows angrier by the moment. He is a judge to be feared rather than loved. And apparently he is a father who tortures and kills his own son to satisfy some legal need for blood.

Look at Christ's death on the cross and you may wonder, "Why did this happen?" The religion of cracked men will answer:

15

"We were born criminals. We entered this world stained with sin and bad to the bone. The moment you took your first breath you were offensive to God, and before you knew right from wrong you were condemned to die. God is just in condemning you because your sin is so great. But he is also kind because he killed his own son in your place. Someone had to be punished to appease his wrath, and better Jesus than you. If you repent for being born, declare your love for this murderous God, you can claim your ticket to heaven where you will spend eternity in his presence."

Is it any wonder so few are attracted to the bad news of dead religion? Who in their right mind would be drawn to such a cruel and sadistic punisher? Thankfully, God is nothing like this.

The gospel of Jesus is infinitely better than the religion of cracked men, for it reveals a God who loves you like a Father. God never changes. He has always loved you and he always will. He loved you when you were a baby and he will love you when you're old. He loves you when you're good and he loves you when you're bad. Your behavior cannot diminish his love for you. This is the true message of the cross.

> But God demonstrates his own love for us in this: While we were still sinners, Christ died for us. (Romans 5:8)

Why did Jesus come and die? Because God loves us and doesn't want to lose us. The cross is not about satisfying some legal need for blood. Nor is it about appeasing an angry deity. The cross is divine retribution against those things that harm God's beloved children. It's your heavenly Father applying the hammer of hard justice to the head of the slaver. The cross is your way out of prison and your ticket to life and liberty.

What is your greatest need?

A few weeks ago we packed up the car and headed out for a family picnic. But I took a wrong turn and we ended up at the wrong place. It was entirely my mistake, but it affected everyone in the car. My wife and children had done nothing wrong, but because of my error they found themselves where they did not want to be. My choice had consequences for the whole family.

That's how it is with us and our forefather Adam. He took a wrong turn and we all ended up where we don't want to be. Instead of picnicking beside the sweet shores of our Father's love, we found ourselves caught up in Satan's rebellion. We would've been safe if we had trusted our Father, but we didn't and here we are. Adam and Eve became the first prisoners of an ancient war and every one of their children and their children's children was born inside a POW camp.

The religion of cracked men says we were born criminals, but the Bible says we were born prisoners to sin. "You were slaves to sin," said Paul. "You were slaves to those who by nature are not gods." Paul is not saying we are captive to some bad habits. His word for sin is a noun, not a verb. Sin is a slaver, a monster, a villain.[2]

It's not that we were born bad — it's that we were born on a sinking ship. God didn't put us there; Adam did (see Romans 5:12). By heeding the serpent Adam condemned himself and his children to death. God tried to warn Adam, but Adam didn't listen. He distrusted God, relied on his own judgment, and drove the ship of humanity straight into the iceberg. With the bulkheads ruptured, sin began flooding the lower decks and death became inevitable. It was one man's decision but we would all pay the price.

Religion says our greatest need is to be forgiven for the crime of being born. But our real need is to get off Adam's sinking ship. Religion says you need to be good. But Jesus says you need to be free (John 8:32).

Why do we need to be set free? Because apart from God we are not free. We may think we are free, but our freedom is an illusion. It's the restricted liberty of a slave or prisoner.

The movie *The Matrix* illustrates this deception brilliantly. In the world of the Matrix the human race is plugged into a virtual reality system that consumes people. Similarly, we are part of a system that deceives and devours. The Bible calls it the "present evil age" and "the dominion of darkness," but in the movie, the character Morpheus calls it a prison:

17

> The Matrix is everywhere. It is all around us ... It is the world that has been pulled over your eyes to blind you from the truth ... That you are a slave, Neo. Like everyone else you were born into bondage. Born into a prison that you cannot smell or taste or touch. A prison for your mind.[3]

Life without God is an inferior reality. It's a life of fear and futility. It's a short trip on a sinking boat. It is not what we were made for.

The natural man may think, "Life isn't so bad," but that's because he doesn't know what he's missing out on. The enslaved life is all he knows. The New Testament writers knew better. Like Morpheus, they had been unplugged from the Matrix and saw life as it truly is. They understood that natural man is alienated from the life of God, enslaved to all kinds of passions and pleasures, and bound by his fear of death.[4]

God made man free but sin enslaved us. Our greatest and most immediate need is to be set free from sin and all its cursed effects — sickness, disease, oppression, poverty, and injustice.

What is freedom? The world defines freedom like this: "If it feels good, do it." But live this way and your appetites, and those who feed them, will control you. You won't be free at all.

Religion defines freedom like this: "Do good and avoid bad." But that way leads to pretending. Live like this and you will end up wretched and religious like the Pharisees. They were the biggest do-gooders of their day, yet Jesus said they were slaves to sin. They thought they were God's right-hand men, but they weren't even real people. They were cartoon characters living little lives and hiding behind masks of religious activity. They were just as bound as the "sinners" they despised.

When Jesus confronted them with the reality of their captivity, they didn't believe him. They said, "We are Abraham's descendants and have never been slaves of anyone" (John 8:33). Yet Jesus insisted they needed to be set free.

> If the Son sets you free, you will be free indeed. (John 8:36)

Know Jesus and you will be free *indeed*. Not fake free. Not merely free to choose which prison bunk you sleep on, but totally free of the slaver called sin.

What does real freedom look like? Jesus shows us, for he lived a truly free life. Jesus lived free from fear, anxiety, sickness and all the other symptoms of sin. He knew what it was to receive love and give love in return. He walked every day in the sunshine of his Father's favor and remained untouched by the corrupting pressures of this present age. His reality was supernatural and he brought heaven to earth everywhere he went. This is the life he offers you. This is the glorious freedom of the children of God.

Who is a sinner?

When the Bible says "all have sinned and fallen short of the glory of God" (Romans 3:23), it doesn't mean all are bad, for the Bible also says some are blameless.[5] It means we're part of a reality that falls short of God's reality. Who is a sinner? It's everyone inside the Matrix. It's anyone who settles for the inferior reality of life without God.

Jesus said, "Everyone who sins is a slave to sin" (John 8:34). It's not our sinning that makes us slaves; we sin because we are slaves. We can't help it. The operating system of this present age is flesh based. It promotes trust in self instead of God. Since anything that is not of faith is sin (Romans 14:23), the system is inherently sinful. It falls short of what God has in mind.

You may say, "I'm basically a good person. I'm not hurting anyone." Adam could have said the same thing, yet he missed the mark spectacularly. The issue is not what you are doing but whether you are becoming the person God made you to be. God had a dream and wrapped your body around it. Life is the adventure of discovering that dream and learning who you really are.

Who rescued us?

If you were a first-century Jew raised on a heavy diet of law and temple sacrifice, it would make sense to describe the cross in the language of sacrifice, as is done in the epistle to the Hebrews (see for example Hebrews 9:26, 10:12). But since you are not a first-century Jew, it makes more sense to describe the cross as a rescue mission, as Paul does when writing to the Gentiles.

> Grace and peace to you from God our Father and the Lord Jesus Christ, who gave himself for our sins to rescue us from the present evil age, according to the will of our God and Father ... (Galatians 1:3–4)

The cross is not about satisfying some bizarre need for blood. The cross is a rescue mission carried out by the greatest team of super-heroes in history, namely, God the Father, the Son, and the Holy Spirit.

> Giving thanks to the Father ... for he has rescued us from the dominion of darkness and brought us into the kingdom of the Son he loves. (Colossians 1: 12a, 13)

Who rescued us? Paul told the Galatians it was Jesus but told the Colossians it was God the Father. Which is it? It was both of them working together. It was a joint effort. In the Garden of Eden the Father delivered the threat, and on the cross the Son carried it out.

What about the Holy Spirit? How does he figure in this rescue mission? Jesus tells us:

> The Spirit of the Lord is on me, because he has anointed me to proclaim good news to the poor. He has sent me to proclaim freedom for the prisoners and recovery of sight for the blind, to set the oppressed free, to proclaim the year of the Lord's favor. (Luke 4:18–19)

Who are the prisoners in need of freedom? We are. Every single one of us. We are also the poor in need of grace, the blind who sit in darkness, and the oppressed bruised by the shackles of sin. Thank God for the Holy Spirit who empowered Jesus to set us free. Where the Spirit of the Lord is, there is liberty.

Do you see now why this religious emphasis on good or bad behavior is irrelevant? You can be a good slave or a bad slave and it makes no difference at all. You're still a slave. A prisoner who reforms is still a prisoner. Inmates on death row don't get time off for good behavior.

Jesus did not come to institute a reform program for convicts. He came to proclaim liberty throughout the land. Christ is our long-awaited year of jubilee. In Christ, the enslaved sons of God are redeemed and get to go home.

What happened on the cross?

The children of Israel were enslaved and mistreated for 400 years. Their deliverance was a prophetic play that parallels our own. In the play, the part of the deliverer was played by Moses, who is a type of Jesus the Great Deliverer.

Moses was special because he was the only Hebrew not owned by Pharaoh. Moses was a free man used by God to liberate a nation of slaves. Similarly, Jesus is special because he's the only human who wasn't a slave. Since Jesus isn't of Adam, he's not part of the slave race. This makes him an ideal savior. When you're locked up *inside*, you need help from *outside*, and Jesus is the very definition of *outside help*. Jesus was constantly reminding people, "I am not of this world" (John 8:23). He was saying, "Since I'm not part of the Matrix I can help unplug you from the Matrix."

In the play, Pharaoh represents the villain: the slaver called sin. You may recall that Pharaoh had no desire to free the slaves. Moses said to Pharaoh, "Let my people go." Pharaoh replied, "It's not going to happen," so God destroyed him. Pharaoh and his entire slave-based system were crushed under the mighty hand of God. After the Red Sea, the Israelites had nothing to fear from Pharaoh. He was dead, his army was drowned, and his corrupt government was ruined.

If the destruction of Pharaoh seems over the top, it's because God wanted to give us a dramatic picture of what he was planning to do to the slaver on the cross.

For what the law could not do in that it was weak through the flesh, God did by sending his own Son in the likeness of sinful flesh, on account of sin: he condemned sin in the flesh ... (Romans 8:3, NKJV)

On the cross, God condemned sin. The Amplified Bible says he subdued, overcame, and deprived sin of its power. Need a picture? Look at Pharaoh rotting at the bottom of the sea. That's what God did to sin. Need another picture? Then consider Sodom and Gomorrah. Those cities were wiped off the face of the earth. No trace of them remains. What God did to those cities is what he did to sin. On the cross, God condemned and obliterated sin once and for all.[6]

But he has appeared once for all at the culmination of the ages to do away with sin by the sacrifice of himself. (Hebrews 9:26b)

Again, this is sin as a noun, not a verb. Jesus didn't put an end to bad behavior; he put an end to sin itself—that enslaving power that kept us bound. How did he do it? The details are a mystery, but here is a clue:

God made him who had no sin to be sin for us, so that in him we might become the righteousness of God. (2 Corinthians 5:21)

Sin had no hold on Jesus, but on the cross Jesus took hold of sin and held tight while God poured out his wrath and fury. I like to imagine God the Father and the Son working like a tag team of wrestlers. When God the Son grabbed hold of sin God the Father launched himself off the top rope and delivered the killing blow.

Why do it this way? Why the cross? Because God couldn't tackle sin directly without killing us all. If he had dropped an atom bomb of judgment on the slaver's home, we would've been vaporized. We would've ended up like Sodom. To save us, God tackled the problem from inside the enemy's camp. He came undercover, disguised in human form; like a slave but not a slave. As a man he confronted the slaver, and as God, he condemned him. It was the consummate act of judgment, total and complete.

What happened on the cross? God abolished slavery. He destroyed the Matrix from within, paving the way for our liberation.

What is the gospel of the cross?

The cross tells us two things about God. First, it tells us he loves us more than he loves his own life. Second, it tells us that if God is for us, nothing can stand against us, not even our sin.

The good news of the cross declares that the power of sin has been completely broken. Our enemy has been disarmed and defeated and our sins have been removed as far as the east is from the west. The implications of this are staggering. It means your sins are no longer being held against you (Romans 4:8). You who were once condemned have been blessed with the gift of no condemnation in Christ Jesus (Romans 8:1). You have been forgiven once and for all time through the blood of the Lamb (Ephesians 1:7), and in Christ your status has changed from sinner to righteous (1 Corinthians 6:11, YLT).

Just as sin had no claim on Jesus, sin now has no claim on you. None. Nada. Zip. Your forgiveness is an eternally unshakeable fact.

The religious may ask, "Are you saying all are now saved?" To which I respond, "Repent and believe the good news!" The kingdom of God is at hand, and through faith in Christ and his perfect work, you get to participate in it. Since the Father has qualified you, your sins cannot disqualify you. The only way you can miss out is if you don't believe it—if you refuse to leave the shattered prison.

The carnal-minded may ask, "Are you saying we can sin with impunity?" To which I respond, "Why would you want to have anything to do with that old life of sin?" The impunity question misses the point. Before the cross, we had no choice; we were slaves to sin whether we were good or bad. But after the cross we have a choice. We can stay in the prison or we can run free. We can live according to the old law of sin and death or according to the new law of the Spirit of life.

In Adam, we had no power to choose. We had to live with the consequences of Adam's choice. But Jesus has done away with Adam's sin and your sin and my sin, and now we get to choose. That's freedom.

> Live as free people, but do not use your freedom as a cover-up for evil ... (1 Peter 2:16a)

You are free to fritter away your freedom, but it would be foolish to do so. Choosing to sin is like messing around with handcuffs and losing the key. It is for freedom that Christ has set you free (Galatians 5:1), so be free. Stay free.

You may ask, "How do I stay free in a world still bent towards sin?" You've got to choose who you will listen to. The devil says, "Look at your sin," but God says, "Look at the Son."

The cross marks the end of your old life. The person you used to be died there with Jesus. The gospel declares that in Christ, you are no longer a sinful son of Adam, but a righteous son of God. So reckon yourself dead to sin and alive to Christ and get on with the joyful business of living the Father's dream. It's what you were made for.

3. What About the Resurrection?

If I ever made a movie about the resurrection of Jesus, there would be one detail I would be sure to include. I'd film Mary coming to the tomb in the early morning and finding it empty. Then I'd show her telling Peter and John the astonishing news. Then we would see the two disciples sprinting to the tomb, followed by a shot from inside showing John's face looking in and Peter pushing past. Next, I'd have a close-up to capture the shock on Peter's face before cutting to show what Peter saw, namely, the detail that gives meaning to the whole scene. This is how John scripts it:

> Then came Simon Peter following him, and went into the sepulcher and saw the linen cloths as they lay and the napkin that had been about his head, not lying with the linen cloths, but wrapped together in a place by itself. (John 20:6–7, KJ21)

The empty tomb was not completely empty. Sure, it was missing a body, and that fact should stop us in our tracks. It is the puzzle that primes us for the good news of the resurrection. But if you were a CSI investigator trying to unravel the mystery of the missing body, you would not have been without clues.

Could this have been a case of grave robbery? You observe the strips of linen lying there and wonder, *Who takes the time to unwrap a corpse?* You note the fine quality of the linen and learn that it was recently purchased by a rich man (see Mark 15:46). Since it is inconceivable that a thief would discard such valuable cloth, you dismiss the hypothesis that the tomb was robbed.

Next you consider the possibility that the disciples stole the body to perpetuate a deception. You recall that the religious leaders and the Romans took steps to prevent this from happening (see Matthew 27:62–66). You observe the large stone, the broken Roman seal, and the spooked Roman guards. *Could the disciples have done this? Could the men who quailed and ran at the cross have found the courage to break the law, over-power a squad of soldiers, and shift a heavy stone?* You dismiss this as unlikely.

Then you notice the detail I would emphasize in my movie, namely, the folded napkin, and you are thunderstruck. The napkin is the clue to the mystery. It tells us there is more going on than meets the eye.

What was in the empty tomb?

In Biblical times there were customs governing how one should act when visiting a Jewish home. As Barbara Richmond explains in her book, *Jewish Insights into the New Testament*, the proper way to express gratitude after an evening of fine food and fellowship was to casually crumple your napkin. If, however, you had an unpleasant evening and wished to express your displeasure, you would fold the napkin and leave it as you found it. A folded napkin was a slap in the face of the host. It was an unmistakable sign that you would never return to his house.[1]

The empty tomb wasn't empty. The fine linen cloths remained to show the grave had not been robbed, and the napkin was folded to send us a message. Knowing that many pairs of eyes would look into the tomb, Jesus took the time to fold the napkin as if to say, "I've been to the grave, I didn't care for it, and I will never return." Jesus, who faced death on our behalf and was raised to new life, will never die again.

The implications of the folded napkin were not lost on John:

> Finally the other disciple, who had reached the tomb first, also went inside. He saw and believed. (They still did not understand from scripture that Jesus had to rise from the dead.) (John 20:8-9)

John saw the folded napkin and realized Jesus had risen from the dead. But at this point neither he nor Peter understood that the resurrection had been foretold in scripture. That revelation came later. But what was the scripture they didn't know? It was this one:

> Therefore my heart is glad and my tongue rejoices; my body also will rest secure, because you will not abandon me to the realm of the dead, nor will you let your faithful one see decay. You make known to me the path of life; you will fill me with joy in your presence... (Psalm 16:9-11)

A few weeks later Peter would quote this scripture in his Pentecost speech (see Acts 2:25–28). By then all the surviving disciples, along with many others, had seen the risen Christ, and what they saw changed them. They literally become different men.

The cowardly Peter, who ran away on the night of the betrayal, *after seeing the risen Lord* became the bold witness who confronted the Sanhedrin and was later crucified for his faith. The skeptic Thomas, who refused to believe the testimony of ten honest friends, *after seeing the risen Lord* became the apostle who took the gospel to Persia and was martyred in India. The unbelieving James, who had tried to silence his half-brother Jesus, *after seeing the risen Lord* became the fearless leader of the Jerusalem church and was thrown off the temple when he refused to deny Christ. The hater Saul, who persecuted Christians, *after seeing the risen Lord* became the apostle of grace who wrote most of the New Testament and was beheaded for his faith.

On the night Jesus died, all but one of his disciples fled in fear. By their actions they denied him. Their message to the world was, "We don't know the man." But after they saw the risen Lord and were filled with the Holy Spirit, those same disciples went to the four corners of the earth and to their deaths declaring, "God raised Jesus from the dead. We are witnesses. We cannot help speaking about what we have seen and heard."

Jesus' death on the cross did not change the disciples. What changed them was the resurrection. It's the same with us. When we see Jesus on the cross we learn that God loves us. But when we see Jesus risen from the dead we realize his love is greater than anything life can throw at us. The resurrection proves nothing can separate us from the undying love of God, and *this* is what changes us and empowers us to walk out of the prison of sin.

What is the significance of the resurrection?

The cross is good, but the resurrection is better. The resurrection matters for at least three reasons.

First, the resurrection proves Jesus is who he says he is. Before he died Jesus told the disciples that he would suffer at the hands of religious leaders. He said they would put him to death but that

27

he would be raised to life three days later (Matthew 16:21). What a thing to say! What are we to make of the one who said it? As C. S. Lewis said, Jesus is either a liar, a lunatic, or Lord. Which is it? The resurrection provides an emphatic answer. Jesus is the risen Lord and the Son of God.[2]

Second, the resurrection vindicates Jesus. It's the verdict of heaven that overturns all the verdicts of the world. The principalities and powers tried to kill Jesus, but God raised him and exalted him to the highest place. The religious types said he was possessed by a devil and tried to silence him, but God said, "He is my beloved Son, listen to him" (see Matthew 17:5). The resurrection of Jesus compels us to take sides. "You crucified him, but God raised him," said Peter at Pentecost. "Maybe you ought to rethink your views on Christ." And on that day 3,000 did.

Third, the resurrection proves God's grace is greater than your sin. On the cross, Jesus bore our sin that we might bear his righteousness. If our sin had been too much for him to carry, he would still be dead and you would still be a sinner.

> And if Christ has not been raised, your faith is futile; you are still in your sins. (1 Corinthians 15:17)

But Christ *has* been raised, proving that any claim sin had against you has been fully settled. The gospel of the empty tomb declares your sins cannot condemn you. In Christ, you have been pardoned for all time.

Before he died Jesus said, "The prince of this world has nothing on me" (see John 14:30). Because Jesus rose, the prince of this world has nothing on you either. All the claims and charges that were against you were taken away and nailed to the cross (Colossians 2:13–14). Your rap sheet might have been as long as your arm but it's gone. This is good news for crooks and criminals and sinners like us. In Christ, we have a complete amnesty and eternal redemption.

> He was delivered over to death for our sins and was raised to life for our justification. (Romans 4:25)

If you battle with guilt and condemnation, see the cross where Jesus carried your sins, and then see the empty tomb, which proves the job is done. There is no sin he didn't carry and no sin he didn't forgive. All your sins were dealt with once and for all at the cross — the resurrection proves it.

You may ask, "But what about the sins I haven't done yet? What about my future sins?" Don't you see? When Jesus died and rose again, you hadn't been born yet. All your sins were future sins.

There is only one cure for sin, and it's the finished work of the cross. Jesus isn't coming to die for your sins a second time. Once was enough. This is the good news of the empty tomb. Because of Jesus, your sins cannot condemn you. Yet you may condemn yourself through unbelief. If you think you have to repent and confess and be good before God will forgive you, you are saying, "Christ's work remains unfinished, the tomb is not empty, and I cannot be right with God unless I do what Jesus couldn't."

It is the nature of the unbelieving mind to act as though the resurrection never happened. But a proper response to grace is to say, "Thank you, Jesus." It's to be like Peter, who saw the empty tomb and was changed. It's to be like John, who understood the good news of the folded napkin and believed.

What is the best thing Jesus ever did?

The gospel is first and foremost an announcement. It is a declaration of something that has happened. But what are we declaring? And what happened? We need to remind ourselves from time to time lest we get distracted from the simplicity that is in Christ.

> Now, brothers and sisters, I want to remind you of the gospel I preached to you, which you received and on which you have taken your stand. (1 Corinthians 15:1)

Here is Paul writing to the church at Corinth. He's fifteen chapters into his letter, he's just finished talking about corporate worship, and he has the following thought: *I'd better remind them about the gospel*. That's kind of strange, don't you think? It's like being three hours into a deacon's meeting and the pastor says, "Now item fifteen on our agenda — remind everyone of the gospel."

Surely the Corinthian Christians knew the gospel. "Doesn't matter," says Paul. "You need to hear it again." And so do we:

> For what I received I passed on to you as of first importance: that Christ died for our sins according to the scriptures, that he was buried, that he was raised on the third day according to the scriptures ... (1 Corinthians 15:3–4)

Here are three important facts of Christ's life: he died, was buried, and rose again. Of these the last is the greatest, for if Christ never rose it makes no difference that he died and was buried.

> And if Christ has not been raised, our preaching is useless and so is your faith. (1 Corinthians 15:14)

Certain men in Corinth were denying the resurrection. They were saying, "The dead aren't raised. There is no hope. This is all there is." Paul wrote to refute their dismal lies. He said, "I saw the risen Jesus and so did 500 other people. He is the first-fruits of resurrection life and all who belong to him will rise" (see 1 Corinthians 15:5–8, 23).

For 2,000 years the resurrection of Jesus has come under attack from godless men. It seems every few years, someone writes a book about how Jesus wasn't raised or didn't really die on the cross. They are merely propagating a lie devised by the religious leaders who put Jesus on the cross in the first place (see Matthew 28:11–15). When we hear these made-up stories we need to remind ourselves of the gospel that declares, "Christ has indeed been raised from the dead" (1 Corinthians 15:20).

> By this gospel you are saved, if you hold firmly to the word I preached to you. Otherwise, you have believed in vain. (1 Corinthians 15:2)

Paul is not saying, "You have to believe and keep believing and never stop believing, otherwise you're not saved," for that would make salvation conditional on your believing performance. He's saying, "If the gospel you hold to doesn't reveal a resurrected Jesus, you are believing in vain."

> Remember Jesus Christ, raised from the dead, descended from David. This is my gospel ... (2 Timothy 2:8).

The resurrection is the heart of the gospel message. It is the climax, the punchline, and the point of everything. We were under the curse of sin and death, but a man from heaven set us free and *proved* our freedom by rising from the dead. This is the good news of the resurrection. "*This* is what we preach, and *this* is what you believed" (see 1 Corinthians 15:11).

Why does this matter? Because a gospel without the resurrection is like a car without an engine—it might look good, but it won't actually take you anywhere. It's a lemon gospel. It won't help you and it certainly won't save you. But a gospel that proclaims the saving power of God and backs it up by pointing to the empty tomb is a gospel that can change your life.

The best thing Jesus ever did was rise from the dead, and he didn't do it. God did it to him. Jesus simply trusted that he would. "Father, into your hands I commit my spirit" (Luke 23:46). The same God who raised Jesus raises us. He lifts us out of the dark prison of sin and sets our feet on the sunlit uplands of his grace. We don't do a thing to make this happen. We simply trust that God does it all.

> And if the Spirit of him who raised Jesus from the dead is living in you, he who raised Christ from the dead will also give life to your mortal bodies because of his Spirit, who lives in you. (Romans 8:11)

The gospel of the resurrection is the announcement of *something that happened* so that *something else can now happen*. Jesus was raised to new life so that you can experience new life in him. This new life is not obtained through hard work and discipline. It's received

31

by trusting in a good Father who delights to share his life with his children.

Which Jesus are you trusting?

The essence of the gospel is "Christ alone." But which Christ are we talking about? Which Jesus are you trusting? Is it the baby Jesus who is celebrated each Christmas? Is it the kind and gentle teacher who was friendly to sinners? Or is it the crucified Jesus we remember when we take communion? This may shock you, but none of these Jesuses can save you. There is only one Jesus that saves, delivers, heals, rescues, and gives new life, and that is the *risen* Jesus, seated at the right hand of God.

> And being found in appearance as a man, he humbled himself by becoming obedient to death—even death on a cross! Therefore God exalted him to the highest place and gave him the name that is above every name, that at the name of Jesus every knee should bow, in heaven and on earth and under the earth, and every tongue confess that Jesus Christ is Lord, to the glory of God the Father. (Philippians 2:8–9)

Dead religion proclaims a dead Jesus and promotes dead works that achieve nothing. But the gospel of God's powerful grace reveals a risen and exalted king with a name that is above every other name. A dead Jesus saves no one. But a risen Jesus who has conquered sin and death and now sits at the right hand of God, interceding for us, is a Jesus you can bet your life on.

It is essential that you see Jesus as risen and exalted above all things. If you don't, you will never experience the new life that is found only in him. Your life will be no different from that of an unbeliever.

Perhaps you have said, "I'll believe him when I see him." Maybe you've been praying for a vision of heaven or some supernatural sign. "Jesus, reveal yourself like you did to Paul on the road to Damascus or show me a miracle, and then I'll believe." It doesn't work that way. The Pharisees saw plenty of signs and wonders yet steadfastly refused to believe Jesus. And not everyone who saw the risen Lord believed straight away. Some doubted.[3]

Seeing is not always believing. And seeing is not the key to being blessed. Do you remember what Jesus said to Thomas?

Because you have seen me, you have believed; blessed are those who have not seen and yet have believed. (John 20:29)

Jesus is talking about us. He's saying those who walk by faith are blessed.

Several hundred people saw the risen Lord and were blessed to see him. But millions upon millions have not seen him with their natural eyes, yet they have been blessed too.

You don't need to see to receive the favor of God. You just need to believe. And when you believe in God's favor you will see it. Why am I so sure? Because the gospel reveals the life-saving power of God for *all* who believe (Romans 1:16).

God is good whether you believe it or not, but you'll never fully experience his goodness unless you believe it.

The Jesus of the gospel is more than alive. He's ruling and reigning from the highest place. Everything has been put under his feet (1 Corinthians 15:27). If you are trusting in Jesus-on-the-cross, your faith is misplaced. Jesus is not on the cross but on the throne. *This* is the Jesus that wants to bless you with salvation power, and *this* is the Jesus we fix our eyes on.

What is the key to my breakthrough?

Bob George tells a story about a man called Stan who battled alcoholism for more than 40 years. Stan had given his life to Jesus, but nothing changed. The drinking continued as before. Then one night Stan came home in such a state that his wife called Bob. "Please come and talk to him." Bob went and was inspired to ask the following question:

Stan, when you accepted Christ, which Jesus did you believe in? ... Did you have in mind an honorable man named Jesus of Nazareth who lived 2,000 years ago in a place called

33

Palestine? ... In other words, Stan, did you accept Jesus the *man*? Or did you accept Jesus Christ the *God* who became a man, who was raised again from the dead?[4]

Stan replied that he had put his faith in Jesus who was a man 2,000 years ago. Bob asked if he was willing to trust in Jesus the living God. Stan said yes and was completely delivered from alcoholism that same night.

What you believe determines what you see. If you don't believe Jesus heals today, you won't experience his healing. If you don't believe he conquered death so that you might enjoy new life, you won't experience that new life here and now. The blessings of grace only come to those who believe.

"But Paul, I believe, yet I am still struggling with illness and addiction. Am I doing it wrong?" No. If you are trusting God for healing and deliverance you are doing it right. Rest in God's promise and let nothing move you.

My point is this: many Christians settle at the cross. They are so grateful for grace and forgiveness that they camp at Calvary and miss the resurrection. They lead others to the cross and no further, and the result is powerless, fruitless Christianity.

Don't camp at the cross—Jesus is not there. Instead, see yourself seated with Jesus who has risen from the dead.

What does this mean in our daily life?

The Bible says that when we confess Jesus as Lord, we are saved (Romans 10:9). Do you know what the word *Lord* means? It means Jesus has supreme power and authority. It means everything in creation has to call him "Sir." When Jesus rebuked the demons and ordered them to go, their response was basically, "Yes, Sir." It's the same with sickness. When Jesus commands cancer and diabetes to go, their response is, "Yes, Sir."

Since you are one with the Lord, you need to have the same mind and speak in the same way. You need an attitude of faith that says, "Jesus is Lord" over my situation. Now Jesus is Lord whether you believe it or not, but it won't do you any good unless you believe it and confess it.

When you proclaim Jesus as Lord over your life, you are setting yourself up for a blessing. You are saying:

Addiction (or illness or circumstance), you have a strong grip on me but the Lord Jesus is stronger still. I cannot defeat you in my strength, but let me tell you about Jesus my God, at whose name every knee shall bow, including yours.

James says, "Submit to God, resist the devil, and he will flee from you" (James 4:7). James does not say, "Submit yourselves to Jesus the gentle teacher." Nor does he say, "Submit yourselves to Jesus the dead Messiah." Teachers and martyrs have no power to deliver you from the grip of sickness and addiction. The key to your breakthrough is submitting to Jesus who is God.

As Stan's story illustrates, the devil doesn't flee from those who know Jesus as a man. But those who know their God shall be strong and do exploits. They shall walk through the fires of life and not be burned (Isaiah 43:2).

A gospel which proclaims the cross but not the resurrection is not the full gospel. A gospel which proclaims a dead Jesus but not a living, all-conquering, ruling, and reigning King Jesus, is not the full gospel. If you want the full gospel, make sure you get the whole story — the director's cut — and not the version that ends at Calvary.

4. By Which Gospel Are You Saved?

Read the Bible from cover to cover and you could be forgiven for thinking that there is more than one gospel. For example, the first words of the New Testament in the King James Bible are, "The Gospel According to Saint Matthew." Read on and you will also find the gospels according to Saints Mark, Luke, and John. That's four gospels right there. But wait, there's more.

Keep reading and you will discover Paul telling the Romans about "my gospel." So it seems there must be five gospels. Or maybe more.

Read all the way to the end and you will encounter the "gospel of your salvation," the "gospel of peace," the "glorious gospel of the blessed God," before finally reaching the "eternal gospel" of Revelation.[1]

Of course, these are all labels for the same gospel. There is only one gospel, and that is the gospel which was known to Paul as the gospel of grace:

> I consider my life worth nothing to me, if only I may finish the race and complete the task the Lord Jesus has given me — the task of testifying to the gospel of God's grace. (Acts 20:24, NIV1984)

What is grace?

Paul dedicated his life to testifying of God's grace, but what is grace? Grace is the love of God reaching down and gathering you in his arms. Grace is the confident assurance that with God on your side, you can't lose. Grace is his strength for today and bright hope for tomorrow. Grace is the end of religion. Grace is the freedom from the unholy need to prove yourself. Grace is divine permission to be who God made you to be. Grace is good.

Those who say grace is one of God's blessings show their ignorance, for grace is not one blessing, but all of them together. Grace is heaven's cure for the world's woes. It's the power of God that turns sinners into saints and haters into lovers. Grace raises the dead and heals the broken. Grace gives strength to the weary and wings to the feeble. Grace is divine.

Grace is the undeserved favor of God. Grace is God honoring us with his presence. In three words, grace is *God with us.*

The angel went to her and said, "Greetings, you who are highly favored! The Lord is with you." (Luke 1:28)

As Mary discovered and we are still learning, we are highly favored. How do we know? Because the Lord is with us. He is not against us, but for us. Jesus is proof of this. God sent us his Son to demonstrate his love and favor toward us.

Grace and truth came through Jesus Christ. (John 1:17b)

Whenever you read the word *grace* in the Bible, you can substitute the name *Jesus* and vice versa. Jesus is grace personified. He is Mr. Grace. What does the grace of God look like? It looks like Jesus. What does the grace of God sound like? It sounds like Jesus. How do we know that God is gracious? Because he gave us Jesus, who is full of grace and truth.

The grace of God comes in many flavors but is ultimately revealed in his Son, Jesus. Jesus is grace, and grace is Jesus.

What is the one and only gospel?

The gospel of God's grace is *the* gospel and there is no other, for a graceless gospel would be no gospel at all. Grace is what makes the good news *good news.*

When Paul refers to the gospel of grace in Acts 20, he means the same thing as when he and others refer to the gospel of Christ or the gospel of God or the gospel of his Son or the gospel of peace. All these gospels reveal the one called Grace who was given to us out of the fullness of the Father's grace and through whom we have received grace upon grace.

"But what about the gospel of the kingdom? Is this a different gospel?" Whenever you hear Jesus talking about the kingdom you can substitute the word *king* because the kingdom is nothing without the king. Who is the King? It's Jesus. So when Jesus says we are to "seek first his kingdom and his righteousness," he is saying, "Seek me and my righteousness." And where do we find his righteousness? In the gospel of grace.

> For in the gospel the righteousness of God is revealed—a righteousness that is by faith from first to last, just as it is written: "The righteous will live by faith." (Romans 1:17)

The gospel declares your heavenly Father loves you and desires to give good things to you. He wants to give you his love, forgiveness, righteousness, and acceptance along with all the blessings of heaven, and all these gifts are found in his Son Jesus.

> And God raised us up with Christ ... in order that in the coming ages he might show the incomparable riches of his grace, expressed in his kindness to us in Christ Jesus. (Ephesians 2:6–7)

To proclaim the gospel of grace is to proclaim the exceeding riches of God's kindness that come to us through Jesus. It is to declare that apart from God, we are poor and needy, but with him we are blessed indeed.

How did Jesus reveal grace?

I am often struck by the things Jesus didn't say as much as the things he did. For instance, Jesus never said the word *grace*. Not once. Since Jesus is grace personified, this is remarkable. It's as if Mozart never said the word *music* or Picasso never said *paint*.

Jesus may not have said it but he surely showed it. His sacrifice on the cross was the greatest demonstration of love and grace the world has ever seen. On the cross he wrapped his arms around a hurting world and gave us a great big hug. That's love. And on the cross he bore our sins and sorrows so that we might be whole. That's grace.

Jesus' whole life testified to the awesome grace of God. On the night he was born, a great company of angels appeared, singing God's praises:

> Glory to God in the highest heaven, and on earth peace to those on whom his favor rests. (Luke 2:14)

Perhaps you worry that God is selective with his favor. "Maybe God will bless me, maybe he won't. I'd better behave myself and hope for the best." Maybe you have prayed, "God, if only you would send an angel to tell me." He already did! He sent a whole company of angels. The angel said this good news was for "all the people" (Luke 2:10). Are you *people*? Then God's favor is for you. Let it rest on you and be at peace.

One of the ways Jesus revealed grace was by proclaiming the indiscriminate love of his Father. Jesus didn't say, "For God so loved the rule-keepers and do-gooders." He said, "For God so loved the *world* ..." God loves everyone. He loves Jews and Gentiles, white folk and colored folk. He loves Catholics and Protestants, cowboys and Indians, gays and straights. God loves *you*.

Jesus demonstrated the radical love of God by hanging out with anyone and everyone. It didn't matter whether you were a big wheel in the synagogue or a crooked civil servant. If you opened your door to Jesus, he'd break bread with you. That's how he rolls, and that's grace.

Another way Jesus revealed the grace of God was by telling stories. Some of his stories were scandalous, like the one about the father who forgave and then partied with his prodigal son. *God is like that?! Incredible!* Others were metaphors freighted with meaning. "The kingdom of heaven is like a merchant looking for pearls of great price" (Matthew 13:45). This seems like a nothing-story until you realize Jesus is talking about himself. He is the merchant who gives up all he has to purchase us his treasured pearl. *You died for me, Jesus? I'm your treasure?! I'm blown away.*

Another way Jesus revealed grace was by showing uncon-ditional forgiveness.

Some men brought to him a paralyzed man, lying on a mat. When Jesus saw their faith, he said to the man, "Take heart, son; your sins are forgiven." (Matthew 9:2)

Jesus seems to contradict himself. Didn't Jesus say we would be forgiven only if we first forgave others? Yet the paralytic forgave no one. There is no record of him forgiving those who had sinned against him. Yet Jesus forgave him anyway. That's unexpected. That's undeserved favor. That's grace.

It's as if Jesus came to show us two ways to live. "You can live under the law where you reap what you sow, or you can live under grace where you reap what *I* sow. Your choice." To the religious and self-righteous, Jesus emphasized the law. "You want to go that route? Fine. But go the whole way and be perfect as your Father in heaven is perfect." But to sinners and the sick, Jesus revealed grace. "You're healed. You're forgiven. Peace be with you."

What is the only thing you can do with grace?

The grace of Jesus does not sit well with our religious urge for self-improvement. Our innate desire to impress God with our goodness collides with his desire to impress us with his. Religion demands that we *try*, but grace inspires us to *trust*.

For God so loved the world that he gave his one and only Son, that whoever believes in him shall not perish but have eternal life. (John 3:16)

Look carefully at the end of that verse. There is a full stop—a period. Thank God for that period! It is the greatest period in the history of periods. That period declares the surprising grace of God. It preempts all the ifs, buts, and maybes. What conditions does Jesus attach to the gift of God? None. The Son has already been given. What requirements must be met before God will bless us? There are none. The blessings have been given and unwrapped. The only thing you can do with grace is respond.

Respond positively to what God has done, and that's called faith. Faith is simply being persuaded that God is good and that he loves you. Respond negatively, and that's called unbelief. It's refusing to receive the grace of a good God. Since we hunger for love and grace, it's actually harder to refuse than receive. You have to push away from the table of his abundance and resist the sweet aroma of his feast. And then, because you are still hungry, you have to work for food that doesn't satisfy. It takes a lot of effort to be an unbeliever.

We were made for grace like we were made for food. Without it we'll die. The good news is that grace is on the table, and there's no cover charge and no dress code. Come as you are and eat what is good.

How do we pervert the gospel of grace?

If you were on a sinking ship and had a choice of going into the water wearing an anchor or a life preserver, which would you choose? I know, it's a silly question. Yet this is the choice we make when we choose which gospel to be believe. Many so-called gospels are preached, but only one reveals God's saving power, and that is the gospel of God's grace.

Tragically, the gospel of grace is not always preached in its pure form. This can leave you confused about your standing with God. In your confusion, you may even abandon God's grace for inferior alternatives. That's like swapping a life preserver for an anchor. As Paul said to the Galatians, it's not a smart move.

> I am astonished that you are so quickly deserting the one who called you to live in the grace of Christ and are turning to a different gospel—which is really no gospel at all. Evidently some people are throwing you into confusion and are trying to pervert the gospel of Christ. (Galatians 1:6–7)

What does it mean to pervert the gospel of Christ? The Greek word for the verb *pervert* can be translated as *turn around*. A perverted gospel is a turned-around gospel. It is a gospel which turns your focus away from Jesus onto something else. If the

42

gospel of grace reveals *Christ alone*, then a perverted gospel is *Christ plus something*. It's the somethings that sink you.[2]

The New Testament writers list many things that can distract you from sincere and pure devotion to Christ. Here are ten:

1. *Human effort, i.e., performance-oriented Christianity (Galatians 3:3).* "Gotta get busy for Jesus. Gotta work for my salvation. Gotta start producing fruit or he'll lop me." Except that you don't, and he won't. The work of the flesh is no substitute for the life of the spirit.

2. *Empty traditions (Colossians 2:8).* "That's just the way we do things around here. If you're going to be a part of us, you'd better get used to it." Traditions are nice, but don't use them to exclude people from the love and grace we all need. Freely you have received, freely give.

3. *Worldly philosophy, like karma (Colossians 2:8).* "God won't reject me, I'm basically a good person. At least I'm no worse than the next guy." Yet your best is not good enough. All have fallen short of God's glory, and none of us stand but by grace alone. Shrug off those smelly rags of self-righteousness and put on the robe of his righteousness.

4. *Angel worship (Colossians 2:18).* "I get heavenly visions. I see angels." That's nice, but don't get distracted. Fix your eyes on Jesus. Haven't you read that angels don't like to be worshiped (Revelation 19:10)? You wouldn't want to make an angel mad now, would you?

5. *Rules and regulations (Colossians 2:21–23).* Smoking will kill you, but it won't condemn you. Drinking to excess is unhealthy and stupid, but Jesus still loves you. Rules and regulations have an appearance of wisdom, but they don't work because we are not rule-keepers by nature. We are the children of God, not robots. We are creatures of faith, not formulas. We were designed to operate from relational trust, not rules.

6. *Self-denial and abstinence (Colossians 2:23).* Self-denial may be good for your budget, but it won't make you holy. Jesus makes you holy. And fasting may make you thinner, but it won't draw you closer to God. In union with Christ, you're already as close as you'll ever be.

7. Endless genealogies (1 Timothy 1:4). So you think you got sick because your grandfather was a freemason? But weren't you adopted into a new family when you believed? Stop holding your future hostage to the past. Talk to your curses about Jesus, who became a curse for us so that we might receive the blessings of Abraham (Galatians 3:13–14).

8. Fables and myths (1 Timothy 1:4). Did Adam have a second wife? Were the Nephilim angel-spawn? Does it matter? I think not. Such controversies do nothing to promote faith in God.

9. Sin consciousness (Hebrews 10:22). If you are more conscious of your sin than you are of his righteousness, it's like saying Jesus' sacrifice was insufficient. The good news is that God's grace is greater than your sin. His worthiness is greater than your unworthiness.

10. Civilian affairs (2 Timothy 2:4). "We've got to win this election for Jesus." Except we don't. Jesus isn't running for office. He's already Lord of all. Jesus said the anxieties of this age and the deceitfulness of riches can choke the word of grace in your life, making it unfruitful. Don't let the temporary cares of this world divert you from the eternal joys of his.

A perverted gospel will burden you with anchors that diminish your trust in Jesus. We are to be Christ conscious, not self-conscious. To the degree you are focusing on *your* sins, *your* behavior, and *your* labor, you are not focused on him. You have been turned around and have fallen from grace.

So ditch the anchors and cling to Jesus with both hands. He is all you need.

What is the whole gospel?

Heaven forbid that we preach half a gospel, but what is the whole gospel? Your answer to this question reveals much about your faith in Christ. For instance, whenever I proclaim the good news of God's unconditional love, I can just about guarantee that some serious person will chide me for not preaching the whole gospel.

What they say: "We've got to preach the whole counsel of God, brother." What they mean: "You should tell people they need to do stuff — repent, confess, turn from sin, work, etc. — to earn the free gifts of grace."

Earn the free gifts of grace?! What an absurd idea. It's like telling your children to pull out their piggy banks on Christmas Day because you expect them to reimburse you for your gifts. How can you compensate God for his priceless gifts to us? There is no way. It would be like Bill Gates giving his fortune to a homeless man and the poor man trying to repay him with a bottle cap. It's ludicrous. What can we give back to God other than our heartfelt gratitude?

"Paul, are you saying we don't need to repent and confess and turn from sin?" Those things are important, but they are not part of the gospel. The gospel is not an invitation for *you to do*; it's an announcement of what *God has done.*

Those who worry that the "whole gospel" is not being preached are basically saying, "There's more to this gospel than grace alone." In other words, grace is not enough. Maybe you were saved by grace, but to stay saved you have to do stuff. You have to pay the fee. You've got to work for the Lord and tithe and witness to the lost. But this is mixed up. It's like telling your spouse, "I married you for love, but to stay married you have to serve me, give me money, and tell others how great I am." What a loveless thing to say.

And what exactly is this whole gospel we are supposed to be preaching? The Bible gives us a straight answer, as we will see, but religion never does. Instead, religion says "it's complicated, you have much to learn, and if you really want to please the Lord you should study Greek and Hebrew." Phooey!

Paul told the Ephesian elders, "I have not hesitated to proclaim to you the whole counsel of God" (Acts 20:27). Some translations say "the whole will of God." The whole counsel and the whole will and the whole gospel are the same thing because God's will and purposes are always good news.

So what is the whole counsel of God that Paul proclaimed? He tells us three verses earlier. The whole counsel of God is "the gospel of God's grace" (Acts 20:24). That's it.

45

"Just grace?!" says the serious man. Yes, grace and nothing but. Not grace-plus-your-confession, nor grace-plus-your-repentance. Just grace.

Here is the last thing Paul said to the Ephesians:

> Now I commit you to God and to the word of his grace, which can build you up and give you an inheritance among all those who are sanctified. (Acts 20:32)

What is the "word of his grace"? It's not the Bible; it's Jesus. Jesus is the Word of God who builds us up and qualifies us to share in the inheritance of the saints. Jesus is the Living Word who testifies to the grace of God.

In essence, Paul is saying this:

> When I came to you I did not hold back from proclaiming the whole counsel of God, which is the gospel of grace revealed in Jesus. And now that I am leaving I want to commit you to the word of his grace, which is Jesus. Do you see my beloved Ephesians? It's Jesus from start to finish.

If you would preach the gospel, the whole gospel, and nothing but the gospel of God, then preach Jesus and nothing else. Jesus is both the will of God and the word of his grace.

So how can we get this wrong? How do we *not* preach the whole gospel? Not by leaving bits out, but by adding bits in.

The grace of God is perfect and cannot be improved upon. Anything we add detracts from its inherent perfection. What do these gospel additives look like? I am sure you know them. They are called prayer and fasting, Bible study, the spiritual disciplines, tithes and offerings, Christian duty, the virtues, works of service, ministry, self-sacrifice, helps, missions, outreach, submission, sowing, etc. In the hands of graceless religion, these good things become death-dealing burdens. If you are being told you must do these things to receive the favor of God—his love, acceptance, forgiveness, healing, provision, deliverance, etc.—you are not getting the whole gospel. You are getting a diluted and contaminated gospel.

Perhaps you've heard people say, "Grace is an important part of the gospel." That's like saying food is an important part of your diet. Grace is not a part of it, but the whole of it. Any part of the message that is not grace is not good news. Anything that distracts you from Christ and his finished work has the potential to turn you around and lead you away from the path of life. Reject it. Insist on the good stuff and commit yourself to God and the word of his grace.

5. Am I Under Law?

Not too long ago Camilla and I were having dinner at a restaurant. We found ourselves sitting under a sign that said, "The Law." The sign declared that anyone intoxicated would be asked to leave the premises. What struck me was that the law had clear jurisdiction. It applied only so far and no further. As long as we were in the restaurant we were under the supervision of the law. But as soon as we stepped outside, the law had no hold on us.

What about the laws in the Bible? Are they universal or do they have limited jurisdiction? Do they apply all the time or only some of the time? Do they apply to us?

> For sin shall not have dominion over you, for you are not under law but under grace. (Romans 6:14, NKJV)

Am I under law? This ought to be the easiest question in the book, for the Bible provides a straight answer. "You are not under law but grace." And just in case you missed it, Paul says it again in the next verse: "We are not under law but grace" (Romans 6:15). This ought to be an easy question, but it's not because many either haven't heard what Paul said or they are slow to believe him.

About ten years ago I was in a meeting and someone asked, "Are we under law, yes or no?" There was a confused murmur of responses. Most people had no idea. So we turned to Romans 6 where Paul clearly says, "We are *not* under law." The question was asked again. "Are we under law, yes or no?" And there was *still* a confused murmur of responses. Even though they had just read the answer in their Bibles, many remained uncertain.

Uncertainty is unbelief, because how can you be confident of that which you are unsure? Paul writes so that you won't have any doubts on this issue. He says, "We are not under law but grace." We are not saved by the law, kept by the law, or supervised by the law. As believers, we are to have nothing to do with the law. It's the grace of God from start to finish.

49

What is the law?

"Paul, what law are you talking about?" What have you got? It makes little difference how you define law. Law is law. The law could be the Ten Commandments or the commands of Jesus. The law could be the exhortations of the New Testament or the unwritten rules of your Bible-study group. "The Law" is anything you must do to merit favor or avoid condemnation.

The world runs on law. At home, in school, and in the workplace, we are rewarded for doing good and punished for doing bad. Much of the church also runs on law. If you are faithful in your service to the Lord, you'll be rewarded for being a good Christian. You'll be recognized as a star, invited to speak, and given positions of importance. However, if you are derelict in your duty, you'll be marginalized, penalized, and ostracized.

The kingdom of God runs on grace, not law. In the kingdom we are not blessed because of what we do but because of who he is. The laws of this world won't serve you in his. In God's economy, all is grace.

"But don't we need the law to know what pleases God." Faith pleases God. Since the law is not of faith (Galatians 3:12), you cannot please God by keeping it. Your choice is clear. You can trust in your own law-keeping performance or you can trust in the grace of God—but you can't do both. Grace and law are exclusive. Mix them together and you'll get the benefits of neither.

"But Paul, the law gives us knowledge of right and wrong." So did the forbidden tree and we weren't supposed to have anything to do with that either. There's more to life than doing good and avoiding evil. Real life is found in relationship with the one who fulfilled all the requirements of the law on our behalf.

The law doesn't save us, sanctify us, or teach us how to please God. So what does the law do?

What is the purpose of the law?

Watchman Nee tells a wonderful story about a clumsy servant. As long as the servant sits still and does nothing, his clumsiness is not apparent. But the moment you ask him to serve, trouble begins.

He knocks over furniture, drops plates, and makes a frightful mess. In Nee's parable, we are the clumsy servant:

> We are all sinners by nature. If God asks nothing of us, all seems to go well, but as soon as he demands something of us, the occasion is provided for a grand display of our sinfulness.[1]

The problem is that we think we're free but we're not. We're prisoners of sin but we don't know it until the law comes along and asks us to do something we cannot do. The law reveals our bondage to sin.

> I know that all God's commands are spiritual, but I'm not … I've spent a long time in sin's prison. (Romans 7:14, MSG)

Picture a prisoner living in a small cell. He's been there so long he's become institutionalized. His cell is all he knows. He thinks it's his home and has decorated it with flowers made out of toilet paper.

Then the law comes along and says, "You think this is real life? Real freedom and flowers are just outside this wall. Pass through and be free." The prisoner says, "I'll do it," and walks smack into the wall. The prisoner remains as confined as ever, but now he's had some sense knocked into him. He sees the stone walls of his cell as if for the first time. He realizes, *This is not my true home. I want to be free.*

We are the prisoners, and our bodies are the prisons. Our bodies aren't inherently evil or sinful, but they are the place where we encounter sin. The effects of sin are felt in our bodies and minds. This is why Paul refers to "sin in me" and "the body of sin."[2]

Since we experience sin in the flesh, the temptation is always to respond in the flesh. But there's a problem. Sin is stronger than our flesh. We may think we can resist sin through sheer determination, but it's a lost cause. This is why we need the law — not to help us win against sin but to help us lose and lose quickly.

Allow me to explain.

The law serves four important purposes. First, it reveals our sinful state. It draws attention to our confinement under sin.

> Therefore no one will be declared righteous in God's sight by the works of the law; rather, through the law we become conscious of our sin. (Romans 3:20)

Before he came to Christ, the apostle Paul had a problem with coveting. But he didn't know he had a problem until the law revealed it to him.

> I would not have known what sin was had it not been for the law. For I would not have known what coveting really was if the law had not said, "You shall not covet." (Romans 7:7b)

It's the same with us. We don't know what sin is until the law tells us. We don't know we're not free until the law dares us to act free and we find we cannot.

You may have thought, "I'm basically a good person," but the law says, "You don't know what good is. No one is good except God alone. You have fallen short of the good life for which he made you. You are less than what God intended you to be." As we listen to the accusations of the law we realize this is true. "I covet. I lie. I slander. I'm not such a good person after all. I'm guilty as sin."

Does the law help me overcome sin?

The second purpose of the law is to inflame sin. Upon discovering he had a coveting problem, Paul resolved to fix it. "I didn't know I was sinning, but now that I do, I'll stop." Problem solved. Only it wasn't. To his dismay, Paul found that his law-keeping efforts only made things worse.

> But sin, seizing the opportunity afforded by the commandment, produced in me every kind of coveting. For apart from the law, sin was dead. (Romans 7:8)

If you have ever tried to overcome sin in your own strength, you will know that the harder you try, the harder it gets. You resolve to be pure but you stumble. You promise to do better but fail again. In exasperation you cry, "I'm such a sinner." Then you hear an inspiring sermon about giving God your best, and your flesh responds, "Jesus, I'll do it for you." So you charge hard at that stone wall like a bull. "This time I'm gonna make it." Bam! Down you go again. "Why is it that the harder I try the harder I fail?" Because you're relying on the flesh and the flesh is weak.

> The law was brought in so that the trespass might increase ...
> (Romans 5:20a)

The harder you try to keep the law, the stronger sin becomes, for the power of sin is the law (1 Corinthians 15:56). The problem is not the law, which is holy, righteous, and good. The problem is you. As sin's prisoner, you are simply not capable of freeing yourself. The harder you run into that wall, the harder it'll smack you. This leads to the third purpose of the law.

> I found that the very commandment that was intended to bring life actually brought death. For sin, seizing the opportunity afforded by the commandment, deceived me, and through the commandment put me to death. (Romans 7:10–11)

God didn't give us the law to help us overcome sin. The law is meant to help sin overcome you. The law ministers death. It does this by demanding we perform day in and day out, with no time off for good behavior. "Come on you sinner! Try harder. Don't you want to do your best for Jesus? Don't you want to be free?"

Urged on by the merciless law, we run into the stone wall again and again until we are smashed and broken and our pathetic promises are exposed as futile. Eventually we collapse, spent and hopeless. From our once-proud mouths we whisper words of defeat. "I can't do this. What a wretch I am. Who will rescue me from this prison of death?"

And this leads us to the fourth and finest purpose of the law.

Why do we need the law?

> So the law was our guardian until Christ came that we might
> be justified by faith. (Galatians 3:24)

The ultimate purpose of the law is to point you to Jesus so that
you may be set free from sin and live in it no longer (Romans 6:2).
The law is not your teacher, your friend, or your protector. But the
law will take you to Someone who is. The law is a guide who
leads you to Jesus.[3]

> For Christ is the end of the Law [the limit at which it ceases to
> be, for the Law leads up to him who is the fulfillment of its
> types, and in him the purpose which it was designed to
> accomplish is fulfilled. That is, the purpose of the Law is
> fulfilled in him] ... (Romans 10:4a, AMP)

If you have met Jesus, the law has fulfilled its purpose. You have
no further need of its aid. You can dismiss it as a good and faithful
servant. Thank God for the law that leads us to Christ.

How do I know if I'm living under law?

The gospel of grace is life-giving water to a thirsty soul. But mix in
a little death-dealing law, and the message becomes toxic. This is
why grace preachers get upset whenever law is preached to those
under grace.

Someone once asked me, "Who's preaching law? I don't know
anyone who is saying we have to live by the Law of Moses."
That's a fair observation. The problem is, Moses wasn't the only
lawgiver. Many are trying to live by the commands of Jesus, the
New Testament, and their own church traditions. We can even
become our own lawgivers by telling ourselves that God's favor
and acceptance hinge on what we do.

There's an easy way to recognize law. You just look for the
word *if*. For example, "*If* you fully obey the Lord and follow his
commands, you will be blessed. However, *if* you do not obey the
Lord and follow his commands, you will be cursed" (see

Deuteronomy 28:1–3,15–16). That's vintage law. It's carrots and sticks for religious donkeys.

In the old covenant, the law was often expressed like this: *If* you listen, *if* you seek, *if* you follow, *if* you obey. The commands may have changed, but religious law today is expressed exactly the same way: *If* you fast and pray, God will act. *If* you avoid sin, he will receive you. *If* you read a chapter a day, you'll keep the devil away. *If* you serve, *if* you give, *if* you go on a short-term mission trip, God will bless you.[4]

There is nothing wrong with serving or praying or any of these things. The problem is the lie that says God's blessings depend on you doing them. That's the old way of the law and it is completely opposed to the new way of grace. In this world there may be seven steps to success or fifteen keys to favor, but in the kingdom of God there is only one and it's Jesus.

The law-based covenant was a temporary arrangement between God and Israel. It was introduced at Mt. Sinai and made obsolete at Mt. Calvary. But many don't know this. They didn't get the memo. They may have heard about grace but they are living under law. Like the Galatians of old, they're trying to walk in two different directions. They're trying to do the right thing in their flesh and they're trying to live in step with the Spirit. It's a recipe for disaster.

Perhaps you feel like the prisoner running into the stone wall. You want to please Jesus but no matter how hard you try, you just can't break free. The problem may not be the sin you're dealing with. It could be that you're trusting in the weak arm of your flesh instead of the mighty hand of his Spirit. It could be that you're living under law instead of grace. Happily, the symptoms of a law-based life are easy to recognize. Here are seven of them.

What are the symptoms of a law-based life?

1. You feel guilty and condemned. Condemnation is the number one symptom of the condemning ministry of the law (2 Corinthians 3:9). It is a sign you are more conscious of your sins than God's grace. The cure for a guilty conscience is a revelation of the new covenant forged in Christ's blood (Hebrews 10:22). It is the joyful discovery that now, in Christ Jesus, there is now no more condemnation (Romans 8:1).

You may say, "I'm not worthy. I've done terrible things." This is the judgment of the law. Stop singing the old refrains of the law and learn the new song of grace. God qualifies the worst of us and clothes us with the robes of his righteousness. A life under law ignores what Christ has done, but a life under grace responds with thanksgiving and praise.

2. *You suffer from performance anxiety.* Anxiety is a typical response to the uncertainty of living under the law. "Have I done enough? Will God be pleased?" The law gives no assurance and demands you do more. Yet the grace of God points you to the finished work of the cross and fills you with confidence and peace. Those who live under law tend to be fearful and insecure, but those under grace abound with joy (Isaiah 12:2–5).

3. *You are conscious of your debt to God.* What debt? Under the law-keeping covenant, it made sense to think of God as a bookkeeper tallying your sins, but your heavenly Father is not like that. Nor does his grace come with a price tag. He is a giver, not a loan shark. God didn't redeem you because he was looking for an indentured servant. He did it because he loves you and longs to display the exceeding riches of his grace to you (Ephesians 2:7).

A life lived under law will always be conscious of some obligation or expected pay back. "I have to prove I was worth it." No you don't. You need to renew your mind, repent of your self-consciousness, and fix your eyes on the author and finisher of your faith. God gave you his Son. How can you pay him back? Instead of trying to repay him for his priceless gifts, why not enjoy what he gave you? Let your life be a shining testimony of the generosity of your gracious Father.

4. *You're not 100 percent certain if you're 100 percent forgiven.* God doesn't do forgiveness in installments. All your sins were taken away at the cross when the Son of God abolished sin by the sacrifice of himself (Hebrews 9:26). Neither God the Father nor God the Holy Spirit remembers your sin any more (Hebrews 8:12, 10:17). The law says, "You must repent and confess before God will forgive you." But grace says, "Turn to God, for he has already

forgiven you." We don't confess to get forgiven; we confess because we are.

True confession, like repentance, is an act of faith. It is a positive response to what God has done. It is acknowledging your need for the grace he has provided in Christ Jesus.

5. *You believe you have a responsibility to serve the Lord.* "Jesus did so much for you, what will you do for him?" This noble-sounding line promotes an attitude of religious duty. It fosters servants when God wants sons. It suggests your value to him is defined by what you do rather than who you are. Worst of all, it trades the intimacy of relationship for the lifeless formality of servitude. Instead of drawing close to your loving Father, you'll be content to be a doorkeeper in the outer courts.

Those under law aren't free to serve; they are obliged to. They work hard but accomplish nothing that lasts. In contrast, those accustomed to walking in the restful rhythms of their Father's grace feel no pressure to perform yet accomplish much (1 Corinthians 15:10). Without any conscious effort, they bear his fruit and change the world.

6. *You mainly think of following Jesus in terms of giving up things.* Christianity is a divine exchange, our life for his. It's true that you cannot follow Christ without renouncing your right to everything, but look what you get in return. We give him our sinful selves and get him *and everything besides* (see Hebrews 1:2). We give up that which we couldn't keep and get that which we can never lose.

If you think following Jesus is mainly about self-denial and personal sacrifice, you've missed the cross. You're operating under the old law of offerings and sacrifice. Do the new math of grace and you will see the numbers don't add up. Not even close. The benefits of grace are scandalous. Christ offers us an unfair exchange, one in which we are greatly favored.

7. *You think, God will bless me as I do my part.* The essence of a life under law is the mindset that says, "I have to do to get." The goal may be salvation or some other blessing but it is nothing more than DIY religion. This mindset is anti-Christ and anti-cross.

Grace and works don't mix (Romans 11:6). Every blessing comes to us through Christ alone. God doesn't bless us in response to our faithfulness, but his. Don't look to yourself and your performance as the source of favor. Look to him.

If not law, then what?

Just as there were two trees in the garden, there are two ways to live. In choosing the forbidden tree, Adam chose independence from God. An independent spirit says, "I will decide for myself what is best." This way of thinking leads inevitably to a set of rules for living. "If I do this, I will be blessed. If I do that, I will be cursed." It's a way of life that seems right to us — it makes sense — but ultimately leads to failure and defeat.

The law-based life is an inferior way to live. It's not the life you were made for. You were created for a relationship based on the unconditional love of your Father. A life lived under his grace has no need for rules for it says, "I will trust him from start to finish. He will lead me in the path of life."

Live by law and you cannot win. The demands are too great and you face them on your own. But live by grace and you cannot lose because God is with you, and he always wins.

Living under law is like being married to a fault-finding husband who constantly criticizes you for your shortcomings but never lifts a finger to help. Living under grace is like being married to Jesus, who is patient and kind, keeps no record of wrongs, and carries you every step of the way.

Stumble under the law and you can expect to be clobbered with the heavy stones of condemnation and guilt. But stumble under grace, and Jesus will cover you with the glory of his perfect righteousness.

The power to change is not found in rules and the brittle promises we make. The only thing that can bring lasting change to a sin-stained world is the supernatural power of God's grace.

6. How Can I Read the Bible Without Getting Confused?

Have you ever read something in the Bible that seemed to contradict something else in the Bible? Have you encountered scriptures that seemed to oppose each other? For instance, David said, "God hates the wicked" (Psalm 11:5), but Jesus said, "God loves the whole world" (John 3:16). Which is it? Job and Hannah both said the Lord kills people (Job 1:21, 1 Samuel 2:6). But Jesus said, "The thief kills; I give life" (John 10:10). Who's right?

If you get your picture of God from Job or Hannah, you'll end up with a different picture from the one you get from Jesus. Or maybe your picture will be a composite made up of bits from all over the Bible. "My God loves the wicked *and* he hates the wicked." Sounds like your God is confused. "My God gives *and* takes away." Yet Paul says God gives without changing his mind (Romans 11:29).

Scriptures that seem contradictory cause some to dismiss the Bible as inconsistent and useless. But Paul said all scripture is useful provided we rightly divide the word of truth (2 Timothy 2:15, 3:16). We divide the word whenever we emphasize one scripture over another. Paul is saying there is a right way and a wrong way to read the Bible.

How do we rightly divide the word of truth?

"The whole Bible is important. If it's in the Bible, I'm going to do it." Well the Bible says we should stone our rebellious sons (Deuteronomy 21:18–21). Do that and you deserve to go to jail.

"That's weird Old Testament stuff. I only do what the New Testament says." Then you're still going to have problems. Jesus said God won't forgive us unless we first forgive, but Paul said he has forgiven us already. Which is it? Who will you believe?

"Obviously I'm not going to listen to Paul. He must be mistaken if he disagrees with Jesus. We should do everything Jesus said." Well Jesus said, "Be perfect" (Matthew 5:48). How's that working out for you?

Everyone divides the Bible one way or another—we all emphasize certain scriptures over others. But how do we divide the word of truth *rightly*? What is the best way to read the Bible? Jesus provides the answer:

> And beginning with Moses and all the Prophets, he explained to them what was said in all the scriptures concerning himself. (Luke 24:27)

Jesus didn't talk about Moses and the prophets so the disciples would have a better understanding of Moses and the prophets. He did it so they would understand him and why he came.

To rightly divide the scriptures, we need to ask two questions. Here's the first one.

What does this scripture mean in light of Christ and his work?

The Bible was written in such a way to confound the wisdom of the so-called wise. It contains scriptures that appear to contradict one another confounding attempts to reduce it to a rule-book or instruction manual. We may be tempted to ignore bits we don't like, but it's better to read the whole book through the lens of Jesus. We need to ask, "How does this scripture help me understand Jesus and what he has done?"

The cross is the key. Before the cross God related to the children of Israel through the temporary law-keeping covenant. After the cross God introduced a new covenant of grace that applies to everyone everywhere.

> By calling this covenant "new," he has made the first one obsolete; and what is obsolete and outdated will soon disappear. (Hebrews 8:13)

The cross marks the crossroads of two covenants. Before he went to the cross Jesus said, "Every sin and blasphemy will be forgiven" (Matthew 12:31). When was every sin and blasphemy forgiven? At the cross.

The cross changed everything. God hasn't changed—he never changes. But the means by which we relate to him and he to us has changed. Consider these contrasts:

— Before the cross we were blessed if we obeyed and cursed if we didn't (Deuteronomy 11:26–28). But after the cross we are blessed because Christ obeyed (Ephesians 1:3), and through him we are redeemed from the curse of the law (Galatians 3:13).

— Before the cross Adam's sin meant condemnation for all (Romans 5:18). But on the cross our sins were carried away, and there is now no condemnation to those who are in Christ Jesus (Romans 8:1).

— Before the cross God was distant and unapproachable (Exodus 19:12). But at the cross the veil was torn, we were brought near to God, and now we can boldly approach the throne of grace (Ephesians 2:13; Hebrews 4:16).

— Before the cross it was important to keep a record of sins (Leviticus 4–5). But after the cross God chooses to remember our sins no more (Hebrews 8:12).

— Before the cross God said, "Thou shalt" (Exodus 20), but after the cross God says, "I will" (Hebrews 8:8–12). In the old covenant, God's favor hinged on your faithfulness. But in the new, his favor comes to us on account of Christ's faithfulness.

— Before the cross righteousness was demanded of sinful men (Deuteronomy 6:25). But after the cross righteousness is freely given to all who want it (Romans 1:17, 5:17).

— Before the cross, God's presence came and went, causing people to hunger for his spirit (Psalm 51:11). But after the cross God makes his home with us and promises to never leave us (John 14:23, Hebrews 13:5).

Read the bits of the Bible that come before the cross and chances are you will be reading about a covenant that never applied to you and no longer applies to the Israelites. Why is this obsolete material in the Bible? Because it helps us appreciate who Jesus is and what he has done. The law is the shadow, but Jesus is the reality. The law is a warm-up act, but Jesus is the star of the show. The law is the prosecuting attorney who condemns you as guilty, but Jesus is the great advocate who sets you free.

When reading the Bible we need to distinguish between the old law covenant, which condemns sinners, and the new covenant of grace, which makes sinners righteous. We need to ask, "Does this passage describe a world looking forward to Christ and his redemptive work or a world looking back?" And once we have answered that question, we need to ask this ...

Who is being addressed?

The second question we must ask of any scripture is, "Who is the writer writing to or about?" Specifically, is this passage directed to those under law or grace? Is it for those who know Jesus or those who don't? This isn't about judging people, for Jesus loves everyone. But not everyone loves him. People divide themselves by their response to truth, which is why Jesus distinguishes sheep from goats. Surely, Jesus loves the goats as much as he loves his sheep, but he has different words for them.

Jesus told the Pharisees, "Woe to you ..." That's a warning for Pharisees, but not for you. Jesus told the Pharisees they belonged to their father the devil (John 8:44). Again, that's for them, not you. You belong to your Father in heaven.

Everything in the Bible is helpful, but not everything is helpful for you. This should be obvious, but it's not. I regularly hear from people who say things like, "The New Testament epistles were written exclusively for churches, so we should do everything in them." This is not true. One of the epistles was addressed to "the twelve tribes" of Israel (James 1:1). Others were addressed to individuals. Is your name Philemon or Titus? Are you part of the twelve tribes?

"Paul, are you saying these epistles are irrelevant?" Not at all. They are very useful, and we can learn much from them. I am saying we need to filter everything we read through Jesus, and we need to consider who is being addressed. James, for instance, says this:

> Now listen, you rich people, weep and wail because of the misery that is coming on you. (James 5:1)

That sounds like bad news for rich people. What will you do with it? How will you divide this word? You may say, "I'm not rich, so this isn't for me." But if you're reading this on a Kindle or if you bought this book with a credit card, then by global standards you are rich indeed. Even if you're not rich you should wonder about Abraham, who was. Is James condemning Abraham? Surely not. So how do we account for James' harsh words?

We need to ask the second question: "Who is being addressed?" Read these words in context and you will see that James is not describing Christians, but the rich and powerful who infiltrate our meetings, exploit their workers, murder the innocent, and slander the name of Jesus. He's talking about corrupt businessmen and officials who trust in money instead of God. And yes, people like that should weep and wail because money can't save you.[1]

Another passage which may trip you up comes from Peter's second letter. This letter is addressed to believers and opens with a heartening "grace and peace be yours in abundance" (2 Peter 1:2). But in the second chapter, Peter goes ballistic. He condemns those who "never stop sinning," cites proverbs about dogs returning to their vomit, and warns of divine retribution.

You may wonder, *What happened to the grace and peace? Why is Peter getting on my back?* But he isn't. He's not talking about you but false prophets and false teachers—those who deny the Lord, are slaves of depravity, and go after the way of Balaam (2 Peter 2:1, 15, 19).

Balaam was an Old Testament goose who knew about God but didn't follow him. Similarly, those Peter writes about are acquainted with the "way of righteousness" (they have heard the gospel) but have turned their backs on it and remain under condemnation (2 Peter 2:3, 21). Since these people are saying Jesus is not Lord, they are definitely not saved. Where are these false prophets and teachers found? They are "among you," says Peter (2 Peter 2:1). They're in your gatherings and on your deacon boards, so beware of them and their anti-Christ talk.

Having warned us about these wolves in sheep's clothing, Peter turns his attention back to us, his "dear friends," in chapter 3. Do you see? You are Christ's beloved and Peter's dear friend. You are not a slave of depravity, so Peter's condemnation of them is not for you. There is no condemnation to those in Christ Jesus.

The only way we can get this wrong is if we confuse the "dear friends" of chapter 3 with the "slaves of depravity" of chapter 2. But we can avoid this mistake by asking, "Who is Peter writing about?" And the answer, in chapter 2, is "not us."

Like Peter, Jude also draws a line between "godless men" who deny Jesus and his "dear friends," who are saved (see Jude 1:3–4). The godless men are not you but are "among you." They're in your meetings and at your "love feasts, eating with you" (Jude 1:12). Some are posing as teachers and prophets. Others are even pretending to be shepherds (Jude 1:12).

We need to wise up to the fact that there are wolves among the sheep. Jude knew this and so should you it. If you don't, you will confuse warnings meant for *them* as warnings meant for *you*.

Jude was not confused. His message is "woe to them" not "woe to you" (Jude 1:11). His rebuke is for the fakers, not the faithful. His message to you is completely different: "Mercy, peace and love be yours in abundance" (Jude 1:2). This isn't rocket surgery. Wolves get warnings; sheep get mercy, peace, and love in abundance. As long as you know who you are in Christ, you shouldn't be confused.

When reading the scriptures it is essential to ask, "Who was this written for or about?" Failing to ask this question is like taking someone else's medicine. Medicine is good, but it might not be good for you.

How do we reconcile contradictory scriptures?

With these two questions in our tool box, we can now begin to reconcile scriptures that seem to contradict each other. Let's start with the example I mentioned earlier:

Jesus: If you forgive other people when they sin against you, your heavenly Father will also forgive you. But if you do not forgive others their sins, your Father will not forgive your sins. (Matthew 6:14–15)

Paul: God made you alive with Christ. He forgave us all our sins … Forgive one another if any of you has a grievance against someone. Forgive as the Lord forgave you. (Colossians 2:13b, 3:13)

Jesus says God's forgiveness is conditional on our forgiveness; Paul says it's not. Jesus says God will forgive you; Paul says he already has. Who's right? Answer: Jesus was, but Paul is.

When Jesus uttered those words in Matthew 6, he was preaching law to those born under law. (How do we know it's a law? The word *If* is a clue.) On the cross Jesus fulfilled the law, and after the cross he changed his message. On the night he rose from the dead, Jesus began preaching unconditional forgiveness (see Luke 24:47). It's important that you see this.

Before the cross Jesus described forgiveness as a verb, but after the cross he described it as a noun. Under law, forgiveness was something God *does*, but under grace, forgiveness is something God *gives*. Forgiveness is a gift, and in Christ you have it.[2]

The cross changed the message. Before the cross it was "God will" but after the cross it became "God has." God dealt with all your sins — past, present, and future — on the cross. You have been eternally forgiven through the blood of the Lamb. So why should we forgive those who sin against us? Not to earn forgiveness (that's law) but to share what we have freely received (that's grace).

Here is another example of two scriptures that seem to contradict each other:

Jesus: For God said, "Honor your father and mother" and "Anyone who curses their father or mother is to be put to death." (Matthew 15:4)

65

Paul: "Honor your father and mother" — which is the first commandment with a promise — "so that it may go well with you and that you may enjoy long life on the earth." (Ephesians 6:2–3)

Both Jesus and Paul are quoting the same law, but they are only quoting half the law. And they're each quoting a different half. Here is the full version of the law:

Honor your father and your mother, so that you may live long in the land the Lord your God is giving you ... Anyone who curses their father or mother is to be put to death. (Exodus 20:12, 21:17)

This law comes with a big carrot (long life) and a big stick (a swift death). Paul mentions the carrot but not the stick; Jesus mentions the stick but not the carrot. Does it matter? I guess that depends on how well you have treated your parents!

Some Christians read the words of Jesus and worry, "I've not honored my parents. According to Jesus I'm in big trouble." Okay, but what about the Ephesian Christians? They never heard Jesus mention the big stick and they didn't have Bibles to tell them. Their only exposure to this law probably came from Paul, who only mentions the carrot.

See the problem? Jesus and Paul are using the same law to send different messages. This leads some to conclude, "Paul missed it. We should follow Jesus." But filter both messages through the lens of the cross and you will see that this would be a mistake. Following Jesus in this instance would actually be dishonoring Jesus and his finished work. It would be like saying Jesus had not fulfilled the law on our behalf and therefore we must.

Recall the second question: "Who is being addressed?" Jesus is talking to Pharisees and scribes (see Matthew 15:1). Are you a Pharisee or scribe? Jesus is speaking on the far side of the cross to those born under law. Were you born under law? No. Then his harsh words for them are not meant for you.

The Pharisees and scribes were law teachers who did not submit to the law. When they condemned the disciples for breaking the tradition of elders, Jesus laid into them for breaking the commands of God.

The heavy yoke of the law is God's gift for the hypocrite. It's for religious pretenders who think they are rich towards God. It is not for you. You have more in common with the saints of Ephesus than the phonies among the Pharisees.

So why does Paul quote the law to the Ephesians who were not under the law? What relevance does this law have for us who are under grace? From a legal perspective, it has no relevance at all. God doesn't reward us for honoring our parents. Paul has just told the Ephesians that all the blessings of God come to us through grace alone (Ephesians 1:3). Nor does God punish us for dishonoring our parents. Paul doesn't mention the big stick because Christ has redeemed us from the curse of the law (Galatians 3:13).

Paul is simply saying that honoring our parents is always a good idea. Whether you're under grace or law, it's a good thing to do. We are not righteous because we honor our parents; we honor our parents because we are righteous. In Christ you are righteous, so act righteous.

Jesus and Paul are speaking complementary messages. They are using the same words for different purposes for different people. There's a wonderful symmetry here. One is using the law to silence the self-righteous, while the other is using it to illustrate a timeless truth. Both are handling the scriptures correctly in their respective situations.

Why should I read the Bible?

I used to read the Bible because I thought it could show me how to navigate life. I considered it *God's Manual for Successful Living*. But the Bible is neither a road map nor an instruction manual. The Bible is a book about Jesus.

The greatest story ever told is about Jesus, who loved us, lost us, and won us back. The Bible tells this story a thousand different ways. Why should you read the Bible? Because it's a good story and you're in it! You are the reason Jesus did what he did.

Read the Bible to learn about Jesus and how much he loves you and who you are in him. Reading the Bible without wanting to know Jesus is like reading someone else's love letters. You might learn a few things about love, but the words won't move you. You won't feel the love.

Some people get confused because they think the Bible has all the answers. It does not. James never said, "If any of you lacks wisdom, you should study the Bible." He said you should ask God (James 1:5). God surely speaks to us through the Bible, but if the Bible doesn't lead you to a revelation of the One called Wisdom, you'll be no wiser than a Pharisee. Of them, Jesus said this:

> You have your heads in your Bibles constantly because you think you'll find eternal life there. But you miss the forest for the trees. These scriptures are all about me! And here I am, standing right before you, and you aren't willing to receive from me the life you say you want. (John 5:39–40, MSG)

Everything in the Bible points to Jesus and his redemptive work. Jesus can be seen in every book and on every page. Although his name doesn't appear in the Old Testament, he is concealed in the stories of Joseph, David, the ark, the Fall, the law, the tabernacle, and even the furnishings used inside the temple. The deeper you look into the Bible, the more you see — provided you're looking for Jesus.

The Bible is the best book on the planet. It's brilliant, inspired, earthly, heavenly, historical, biographical, prophetic, apocalyptic, poetic, and epic. It reveals much about the character and purposes of God, but ultimately it's just a book. A misguided teacher will use the book to tell you what you should do, but a good teacher will use it to show you what Jesus has done and what you can now do because of what he has done.

Since there is no better teacher than the Holy Spirit, a good way to read the Bible is to read slowly and ask questions. "Lord, what does this mean? How does this scripture reveal you and your good purposes? Show me what you want me to see. Help me to become who you made me to be."

Reading without relationship is pointless. You'll never get anything out of the written word unless your aim is to know the Living Word. Don't read the Bible because you're supposed to or because it pleases God. Read the Bible to know him more and to discover the good things he has in store for you.

What is the best translation of the Bible?

People often ask me, "What is the best Bible translation?" Easy question. Jesus is. He is the Living Word of God and he is flawless and free of translation errors. If you want to know more about the character of God and his eternal purposes, study Jesus.

However, I appreciate my answer is not helpful to those who are choosing a Bible. In that case, I have another answer. If you are looking for the perfect translation, allow me to end your quest now. There isn't one. All translations have biases and inaccuracies.

Finding the right Bible is like finding the right spouse. Don't look for the perfect man or woman—you'll never find one. Instead, find the one who is perfect for you.

Which is the best version of the Bible? It's the one you actually read. If you bought a particular translation because it came highly recommended, but it now sits gathering dust on your shelf, then that translation is not the perfect Bible for you.

An unread Bible is a useless Bible. So find a Bible that speaks your language, resonates with your spirit, and strikes you as beautiful to read. That's the best translation for you.[3]

7. Should I Do Everything Jesus Said?

In my experience, the greatest barrier some have to believing the gospel of grace is they are confused by some of the teachings of Jesus. They hear, "grace, grace, grace," and the lights start to go on. But then someone reminds them of a conditional statement made by Jesus, and the shades go back up. Suddenly the grace of God doesn't seem so free. It's unconditional love—with conditions.

"But if Jesus said it, shouldn't we do it?" Well that depends on what he said, to whom he said it, and why he said it. This may come as a surprise, but not everything Jesus said was meant for you.

In many Bibles the words of Jesus are printed in red letters. "Don't stray too far from the red letters" is a piece of advice often given to new believers. It means stay close to the teachings of Jesus and you can't go wrong. It sounds good, but it's actually bad advice.

Read the red letters of Jesus and you will find two medicines: grace and law. Jesus gave grace to sinners and law to the self-righteous. Like a perfect physician, Jesus gave people exactly what they needed. This is confusing to some. They wonder, *Which medicine is for me? I like grace, but the commands of Jesus are hard to ignore.* In their confusion, they drink both medicines. They swallow grace and law and end up receiving the benefits of neither.

Living by the red letters of Jesus is a bit like swallowing whatever you find in the medicine cabinet. If you fail to distinguish his life-giving words of grace from the death-dealing words of law, you could hurt yourself. We'll look at the dangers of mixing law and grace in the next chapter. But in this chapter we will look at some of the hard-to-swallow teachings of Jesus.

Did Jesus live under law or grace?

Jesus lived at the crossroads of two covenants. As humanity's representative he came to fulfill the old law-keeping covenant so that we might relate to God through a new and better covenant forged in his blood. Since the new covenant could not begin before he died (see Luke 22:20), Jesus lived all of his pre-cross life under the old covenant of the law.

> But when the set time had fully come, God sent his Son, born of a woman, born under the law, to redeem those under the law, that we might receive adoption to sonship. (Galatians 4:4–5)

Jesus was born under law, circumcised by law, and presented in the temple according to the law. Every Jewish person Jesus met was also born under law. To those born under the law, Jesus said this:

> The teachers of the law and the Pharisees sit in Moses' seat. So you must be careful to do everything they tell you. (Matthew 23:2–3a)

Jesus spoke two languages. To those born under the law, he spoke the language of the law. But to those not under law—Gentiles, you, me, and everyone born after the cross—Jesus speaks the language of grace.

It is essential that you understand this. Jesus lived under the law, but on the cross he fulfilled all the requirements of the law so that we might live under grace. It's a whole new way of life with a whole new language.

How did Jesus preach the law?

Jesus is grace personified. In chapter 4 we looked at some of the ways Jesus dispensed grace. But Jesus was also the greatest law-preacher of all time. This is not obvious but it's true. When religious people came to trap him with theological puzzles, Jesus would typically respond with the law. "What did Moses command you?" (Mark 10:3). To the Jews in the temple, Jesus said:

> Has not Moses given you the law? Yet not one of you keeps the law. (John 7:19a)

Nobody preached the law like Jesus. Consider this passage:

> For if you forgive other people when they sin against you, your heavenly Father will also forgive you. But if you do not forgive others their sins, your Father will not forgive your sins. (Matthew 6:14–15)

This is one of the most popular sayings of Jesus. It is also vintage law and a killer scripture. It is not good news. This verse should make us shudder, for it says our forgiveness rests on our ability to forgive others. This is bad news because we are poor forgivers indeed. People sin against us repeatedly. Have we honestly forgiven them all? What if we miss one?

And what do we say to those who have been abused and mistreated? What do you say to a child who has been molested? "Sweetie, you need to forgive that evil man, otherwise God won't forgive you." That's not grace. That's the condemning ministry of the law in full bloom. How do you forgive the unforgivable? You can't. Then you're in trouble, for the law condemns you as an unforgiver.

The law is any conditional statement that links our behavior with blessings or curses. It's tit for tat and *quid pro quo*. How do we recognize the law that Jesus preached? Just look for the carrots and sticks. You will find plenty in the Sermon on the Mount.

> Do not judge, or you too will be judged. (Matthew 7:1)

That's good advice but it's also law. It comes with a big stick (judgment). Here is another example:

> But I tell you that anyone who is angry with a brother or sister will be subject to judgment … And anyone who says, "You fool!" will be in danger of the fire of hell. (Matthew 5:22)

This is not good news. It's bad news for anyone with a brother or sister. It's pure law. There is no grace here, just condemnation.
Here is another tough saying of Jesus:

73

If your right eye causes you to sin, pluck it out and cast it from you; for it is more profitable for you that one of your members perish, than for your whole body to be cast into hell. And if your right hand causes you to sin, cut it off and cast it from you; for it is more profitable for you that one of your members perish, than for your whole body to be cast into hell. (Matthew 5:29–30, NKJV)

Chop off your hand?! Was Jesus serious?

This is one of those passages that causes you to do a double-take. *What?! Did Jesus really say that? Was he serious?*

Perhaps you think Jesus wasn't serious. After all, Jesus is the kindest person there is. He healed the sick and touched lepers. Surely he doesn't want us to go around maiming ourselves. Nevertheless, the question stands: Did Jesus mean what he said? Was he being literal or figurative?

"Obviously Jesus wasn't being literal. He is using strong words to warn us about the seriousness of sin. He's not preaching self-mutilation but self-denial. He's telling us we should do whatever it takes to avoid hell."

That's a common interpretation, but there are two problems with it. First, it assumes that Jesus was exaggerating and Jesus never exaggerated. Preachers sometimes exaggerate to make a point, but Jesus always meant what he said and said what he meant. He is Truth personified. It is inconceivable that he would play with words for the crude purpose of ramming home a lesson.

The second problem with this interpretation is it suggests we can do things to avoid hell. Maybe we don't have to self-amputate, but we can confess, abstain, renounce, and generally be good. There's nothing wrong with being good, but if you think you can save yourself by being good then, forgive me, you're as dumb as a Pharisee.

"Wait a second, Paul. Are you suggesting Jesus was being literal? That he really wants us to self-amputate?" Yes to the first question and no the second. Of course, Jesus does not want us to chop off our hands. We are sanctified by the blood of the Lamb, not our severed limbs (Hebrews 10:29). Self-mutilation does nothing to deal with sin, for sin is conceived in the heart not the hand (Matthew 5:28). Besides, if you chop one hand off, you're left with another. You can still sin!

So what's going on here? Why would Jesus tell us to do something he doesn't really want us to do? He's doing it so that we may appreciate the absurdity of trying to impress God with our acts of self-righteousness. "You want to live by law?" says Jesus. "Fine. But if you persist in this pathetic course of self-reliance, you had better be prepared to go the whole way, even if it means sacrificing an eye or a hand."

Was Jesus serious? You bet he was. Salvation is a serious business. You risk much by trusting your own self-righteous performance.

Does Jesus want us to amputate our own limbs? Not at all. Jesus is not preaching the law because he wants you to keep it. He's laying down the law so that you will stop pretending you are.

Why did Jesus preach the law?

Like every grace-preacher, Jesus esteemed the law and the purpose for which it was given. The law was given to silence every mouth and hold the whole world accountable (Romans 3:19). The purpose of the law is to make us conscious of sin and reveal our need for a Savior.

Since Sinai, the Jews had had fourteen centuries to learn what the law would teach them — that we are incapable of dealing with sin. However, the law-teachers and Pharisees had diluted the Law of Moses with their traditions and interpretations. By honoring their traditions ahead of the law, they emptied the law of its power to condemn. As a result, the menace of sin was not fully recognized, and the self-righteous weren't silenced.

If the law had been allowed to do its proper work, the Jews would have been primed and ready for a Savior. But since the law-teachers had been negligent, Jesus had to do their job before he could do his own. Before he could save the world from sin, he had to preach the law that makes sin utterly sinful.

The law is not a standard to live up to. It's a mirror that reveals our shortcomings. In the Sermon on the Mount, Jesus polishes the mirror. He takes the knocked-down law and raises it higher than it has ever been before. "You have heard it said … but I say unto you …"

Why did the Lord of grace preach the law? Because some people will never appreciate the good news until they've heard the bad news, which is this:

> Unless your righteousness surpasses that of the Pharisees and the teachers of the law, you will certainly not enter the kingdom of heaven. (Matthew 5:20)

The Pharisees and law-teachers were good men, but Jesus said they were not good enough. They prayed, fasted, and traveled over land and sea winning converts, but Jesus said they fell short of God's righteous standard. They would never enter the kingdom.

Jesus' words are sobering. You may ask, "If they can't make it, who can?" The brutal answer is no one. All fall short.

You may say, "I'm a decent person. I've never killed or committed adultery. Surely God will let me in." And Jesus replies, "Your best is not good enough. God demands perfection and nothing less."

This is bad news for imperfect people like you and me. None of us lives up to God's standard 24 hours a day, 7 days a week. Look into the mirror of the law that Jesus preached and you will be left with no uncertainty: "I'm a lawbreaker. I'll never get in."

Now you're ready to hear the good news:

> Do not think that I have come to abolish the Law or the Prophets; I have not come to abolish them but to fulfill them. (Matthew 5:17)

Jesus preached the law so that you might appreciate grace. He outlined the high and lofty requirements of the kingdom so that you would abandon your futile quest to qualify. He proclaimed God's perfect standards so that you would trust him who fulfilled the law on your behalf.

Is Christ the end of the law for you?

The bad news of the law declares, "You are not perfect," and the good news of grace responds, "But you have a high priest who is."

Therefore he is able to save completely those who come to God through him, because he always lives to intercede for them. Such a high priest truly meets our need — one who is holy, blameless, pure, set apart from sinners, exalted above the heavens. (Hebrews 7:25-26)

The law will leave you wondering, "Have I done enough? Am I good enough? Am I saved?" But grace gives you the confidence to declare, "Jesus has done it all. Jesus is good enough. Jesus saves me to the uttermost."

This is why we should not read the so-called commands of Jesus as *laws that must be kept*. Jesus preached law so that you would run to grace. You cannot trust his grace *and* your law-keeping. It's one or the other, not both.

Christ is the culmination of the law so that there may be righteousness for everyone who believes. (Romans 10:4)

The gospel of grace declares that the righteousness you and I need comes to us as a free gift (Romans 1:17, 5:17). You are not counted righteous because you keep the commands of Jesus. You are judged righteous through faith in Christ alone.

Should we do everything Jesus said?

"We should do everything Jesus said" is a reckless claim made only by hypocrites. I guarantee those who say we should do everything Jesus said aren't doing everything he said. They're only doing some of the things he said. How do I know? Because they have retained all of their limbs and eyeballs. They're picking and choosing from the words of Jesus. Those sayings which are too hard they dismiss as figurative. "Jesus didn't really mean that." They're like the Pharisees who kept the easy laws and rewrote the hard ones.

Doing everything Jesus said is like ticking every possible response in a multiple-choice test. (You won't pass.) It's driving with both feet on both pedals. (You won't go far.) It's marrying two people at once. (You won't be happy.)

"Paul, are you saying we should not live by the law Jesus preached?" Well, if you do, you are declaring your unbelief in the grace Jesus revealed. You are saying, "Jesus is not the end of the law for me. I don't trust his finished work." This is unwise. It is trampling underfoot the blood of the covenant and insulting the spirit of grace.

"We must do everything Jesus said" is a statement of unbelief. It's saying, "I trust what I do, not what he did."

Can we ignore the teachings of Jesus?

"Grace-teachers claim the words of Jesus are not relevant for us and can be rejected as old covenant teaching." This is a common accusation made against those who preach the gospel of grace. Apparently, we don't take the words of Jesus seriously. In fact, the opposite is true. Those who value grace are the *only* ones taking Jesus seriously.

When Jesus is preaching law, we say that's serious law and not something to be dismissed as hyperbole. If Jesus said it, he surely meant it. And when Jesus is revealing grace, we bow in breathless gratitude. We would not dare to sully his grace with qualifiers and caveats.

Everything Jesus said was good, but not everything he said is good for you. The question of relevance is determined by context. For instance, Jesus had much to say to the Pharisees, whom he called sons of hell (Matthew 23:15). You are not a son of hell, so why would you heed words meant for them? Jesus also spoke to the devil. You are not the devil, so why would you heed words meant for him?

Should we dismiss the pre-cross sayings of Jesus as old covenant teachings meant for another people in another time? This would be a mistake. It would be like throwing away treasure. If all scripture is useful for training in righteousness (2 Timothy 3:16), then the words of Jesus must be especially useful—even his words to the Pharisees.

How should we read the words of Jesus?

Jesus is the greatest preacher of all time. He told stories and preached sermons the whole world needs to hear. The genius of Jesus is that he often preached one message with two punchlines. If you were confident of your own righteousness, you got law, but if you were not, you got grace.

Consider Jesus' story of the Pharisee and the tax collector (Luke 18:9–14). Both men went to the temple to pray. The Pharisee stood up and prayed about himself. His prayer was a résumé. He thanked God that he was not like other men and bragged about his fasting and tithing. But the tax collector stood at a distance and prayed just seven words: "God, have mercy on me, a sinner." Jesus ends the story with a bombshell: "The tax collector went home justified before God."

How does this parable make you feel? Does it fill you with joy or resentment? Your response to the story is your response to the gospel. If you identify with the sinful tax collector, then this story is good news. *Really? He went home justified?* That's the scandal of grace right there. God justifies sinners (Romans 4:5). Search the parable for evidence of the tax collector's good works or merit, and you'll find nothing. Grace is for the undeserving. It's for those without résumés.

But if you are confident of your self-righteousness, this story is not good news at all. "Wait a second. I fast. I tithe. I am better than other people. Jesus, what are you saying?" Jesus doesn't mince his words. "Everyone who exalts himself will be humbled" (Luke 18:14). That's a hard word for a hard heart. It's a word that condemns the self-righteous and silences the boastful. It's a word of law for those who don't see their need for grace.

Jesus is brilliant at giving people exactly what they need. Consider the parable of the prodigal son (Luke 15:11–32). Some people love this story, others hate it. I've had people tell me, "I feel bad for the older brother. He worked so hard." They say this because *they* are working hard. They are good and decent and can't understand why Jesus would throw a party for prodigals and not for them. It troubles them that we are inside whooping it up while they're outside working on their résumés.

The story is real. Every one of us is in it and everyone is invited to the party. Grace is for all. But you're going to have trouble receiving it if you think of your heavenly Father as an employer. And that's the whole point. You're going to have to change your mind about God or you will never enjoy his love.

Words mean different things to different people. If you identify with the tax collector or the prodigal, the words of Jesus are packed with radical grace. You'll read them with praise and thanksgiving and whoops of joy. But if you identify with the Pharisee or the older brother, his words are extremely unsettling. They are serious words, not fun at all. Yet if you allow them, the words of Jesus will change you. They will strip you of your religion and reveal your need for grace.

Let me finish with one more example that reveals the genius of Jesus:

> Be perfect, therefore, as your heavenly Father is perfect. (Matthew 5:48)

If you are standing on your own righteousness, that's pure, glorious law. Jesus is giving you a standard to live up to: perfection. Good luck meeting his standard! If you insist on living by the commands of Jesus, keep *this* command. And if you can't don't bother looking for a loophole. You won't find one. You cannot be mostly perfect. You have to be perfectly perfect—as perfect as your heavenly Father is perfect. The moment you slip up, you become imperfect and you will be condemned as a failure. The sooner that happens the better, because maybe then you will see your need for grace.

However, if you are standing on his righteousness, then these words of Jesus are pure, sweet grace. They will cause you to sing and shout for joy because Christ is perfect, and, in him, so are you. As a result of his perfectly perfect sacrifice, you have been made perfect forever (Hebrews 10:14).

Perfection is not something to strive for, it's something to receive, and in Christ, you have it. Everything about Jesus is perfect—his righteousness, holiness, and redemption are utterly flawless in every way. Since we have received Christ, we have received his perfection. The exhortation to be perfect means "be who you are in Christ." Work out what he has put inside you. Don't focus on your imperfections, but see yourself clothed in his glorious perfections. Put off the old man and put on the new. Be who he has made you to be.

See the difference? One verse, two messages. There's bad news for those trusting in themselves and good news for those trusting in Jesus.

How should we read the words of Jesus? The wrong way is to treat them as keys to life or sacred commands that must be obeyed *or else*. Don't idolize the words; worship Jesus. Read the words through the lens of the cross. Read them to hear Jesus and to receive from the abundance of his grace.

8. Am I Lukewarm?

Many Christians are troubled by Jesus' words to the Laodiceans. They shouldn't be; they're not Laodiceans. As we will see in this chapter, Jesus has harsh words for them but wonderful words for us. Let's start by looking at the harsh words.

> I know your deeds, that you are neither cold nor hot. I wish you were either one or the other! So, because you are lukewarm — neither hot nor cold — I am about to spit you out of my mouth. (Revelation 3:15–16)

What does it mean to be lukewarm? Many think Jesus is talking about apathy or a lack of zeal. "It's better to be on fire for God or coldly opposed to him than halfhearted in the middle." The implication is if you're not full on for God, he will reject you as unworthy. In other words, getting into the kingdom is like trying to get a job at Google: Only the enthusiastic need apply.

This interpretation has become so widely known that the term lukewarm has become synonymous with apathy and complacency. But is that what Jesus is saying here? Is Jesus firing up the troops like a sergeant major? He is not.

Do we get points for enthusiasm?

If Jesus is calling us to be zealous for God, then we have three serious problems. The first is that zeal is a subjective term. No matter how zealous or enthusiastic you are, there will always be someone more zealous who makes you look lukewarm by comparison. You lead two people to Jesus, but they lead a hundred. You fast monthly, but they fast weekly. You go on a short-term mission trip to Canada, but they relocate their family to a nation that persecutes Christians. On your own, you appear to be a pillar of the church. But compared to them, you're a lukewarm slacker. You'll wonder, "Am I doing enough? Will Jesus spit me out?"

But don't panic because it won't be long before you meet someone who is doing less than you. "I'm no Billy Graham, but compared to this person, I'm hot, hot, hot!"

These are silly examples because this is a silly way to think. It is the nature of the Pharisee to make comparisons — "Thank God I am not like other men" — but God doesn't grade on a curve. His standard is perfection, and all of us fall short — even that zealous missionary who took his wife and kids to Taliban country. Religion deals in relatives, but God deals in absolutes.

Defining lukewarm-ness in terms of your performance will make you insecure about your standing with God. This leads to the second problem: a call for more zeal promotes dead works.

The lukewarm-ness of the Laodiceans put them in danger of being spit out or rejected by the Lord. No one wants to be rejected by Jesus, so the usual implication is that you should be *doing more stuff*. You gotta pray more, witness more, travel more, volunteer more, study more, and give more.

But think about this for a second. Since when did we buy into the idea that our works make us pleasing to God? This is self-righteousness straight from the tap. Jesus is not calling for works because that would amount to an admission of defeat. It would be like he was saying, "My work remains unfinished," or "I'm the author but not the finisher of your faith." How absurd.

To try and improve upon the perfectly perfect and completely complete work of the cross is to repeat the mistake of the Galatians. This is what Paul said about them:

Only crazy people would think they could complete by their own efforts what was begun by God. (Galatians 3:3, MSG)

The Contemporary English Version translates Paul's words like this: "How can you be so stupid?" The Darby Bible says this: "Are ye so senseless?" In the words of the Bible, those who trust in human effort are crazy, stupid, and senseless.

Contrary to what you may have heard, we are not in a Mr. Enthusiasm contest. God is not watching to see if you are hotter or more zealous than your brothers or sisters, and Jesus isn't going to spew you out if you don't hand out a gazillion tracts. Carnal zeal gets you nowhere with God.

The third problem with defining lukewarm-ness in terms of zeal is that Jesus says we're better off cold. Either hot or cold is good, but lukewarm is bad. If Jesus is talking about enthusiasm, why would he say it's better to have none than some? Why is it better to do nothing than something? This doesn't make sense.

Some define cold as being totally opposed to God. "It's better to be wholly hostile to God than in two minds." I know theologians excel in the art of making dumb ideas sound plausible, but this one takes the cake. Why would Jesus wish anyone to be opposed to God? This makes no sense either.

What does it mean to be lukewarm?

Lukewarm is what you get when you mix hot and cold. Being hot or cold is good, but lukewarm is bad. Jesus is saying, "I wish you were one good thing (hot) or the other (cold) but not both mixed together (bad)."

Now what are two good things that, if mixed together, give you something bad? Here's a hint: What were the Galatians mixing together? Answer: law and grace. Grace is good and the law is good, but mix them together and you'll end up with something toxic.

Why does Jesus say it's better to be cold than lukewarm? Because if you live under the stone-cold law, you will quickly recognize your need for the grace that flows from the white-hot love of your Father's heart. The law is good because it leads you to Jesus.

Why is it bad to be lukewarm? Because if you mix law with grace you'll reap the benefits of neither. Dilute the law and you diminish its power to condemn. Dilute grace and you diminish its power to save. Do you see? We need unadulterated law to reveal our great need, and we need pure, untainted grace to receive from his great supply.

The Pharisees were lukewarm because they diluted the law. They took the hard laws and made them easier. They emptied the law of its power to condemn and so did not recognize their need for grace.

The Galatians were lukewarm because they diluted grace. They took the favor of God and mixed it with a little circumcision law. They knew that we are saved by grace but they didn't know we are also kept by grace.

Are you lukewarm? You are if you think you can impress God with your law-keeping performance or if you think God gave us grace to help us keep the law. Don't you see? You can't live under both grace and law any more than you can have a hot and cold shower. It's one or the other, not both.

What does mixture look like?

Lukewarm religion is the result of mixing that which cannot be mixed. But what does mixture look like? For the Galatians it was grace plus circumcision, but today mixture appears in subtler forms.

Mixture is price tags on the gift of grace. It's a little law but not the lot. It's unconditional love with conditions. It's unmerited favor you have to work for.

Here's an example of mixture I have heard preached:

Favor is found by serving. Your job is to obey; God's job is to bless. If you're not serving, you're not experiencing favor.

In other words, you have to obey before God will bless you with his grace and favor. That's mixed up. It's prostituting the love of God for the price of service. It's a monstrous attempt to manipulate a response from the Maker of heaven and earth. That's not faith; it's Frankenfaith.

God doesn't bless us in accordance with our works of service but in accordance with the riches of his grace. If you don't believe me, look to Jesus, who is the greatest blessing God has ever given us. How much service had you done before Jesus died for you? None. If God gave us his Son while we were yet sinners, what will he withhold from us now?

The gospel declares we have been blessed with every blessing in Christ Jesus (Ephesians 1:3). All the blessings of God come to us through Jesus alone. No blessing comes any other way. "But Paul, we need to serve and obey in order to *experience* God's blessing." That's simply not true. The only requirement for experiencing God's favor is wanting it. Grace isn't given to those who work, but those who believe.

Don't drink the toxic cocktail of mixture. Don't fall for the lie that says grace is for sale. Jesus shares the stage with no man. His is a perfect work. Our works do not improve it. If you are feeling pressured to perform for Jesus, hear the good law, which says, "You can never do enough," and then hear the good news of grace, which declares, "But Jesus has done it all!"

What makes Jesus sick?

God never makes us sick, but did you know it's possible for people to make him feel sick? This is the reaction the Laodiceans elicited from Jesus.

> So then, because you are lukewarm, and neither cold nor hot, I will vomit you out of My mouth. (Revelation 3:16, NKJV)

Many Christians worry that Jesus will reject them and spew them out of his mouth. Perhaps this is something that troubles you. Don't worry. It's not going to happen. You are part of the body of Christ. Jesus doesn't vomit out body parts.

So what makes Jesus nauseous? A good way to tackle this question is to think about all the people Jesus met when he walked the earth and ask, "Who made Jesus sick?" Was it the sinful? No. Jesus is a friend of sinners. Was it those living meekly under the law? No. Jesus loved those who made an honest attempt to live by the law (see Mark 10:21). Was it those who had faith but no law? No. Jesus marveled at such people (see Luke 7:9). Was it his disciples, who were sometimes thick-headed and carnal? No. Jesus loved his disciples and called them his friends (John 15:12–15).

So who made Jesus sick?

> Woe to you, scribes and Pharisees, hypocrites! For you are like whitewashed tombs which indeed appear beautiful outwardly, but inside are full of dead men's bones and all uncleanness. (Matthew 23:27, NKJV)

Nothing nauseated Jesus like religious hypocrites who prescribed rules which they themselves did not keep.

The Pharisees liked to cast themselves as God's men, busy with God's work, but they were phonies. Their high regard for the law was little more than lip service. Jesus wasn't fooled. He knew that if they had been honest about the law they would've been silenced by it (see Romans 3:19). Yet the Pharisees were outspoken and proud. They strutted around exalting themselves while criticizing others for not being as good as they were. This hypocrisy made Jesus furious.

> You snakes! You brood of vipers! How will you escape being condemned to hell? (Matthew 23:33)

No one would deny the Pharisees were zealous for God. But theirs was a carnal zeal based on the lie that says we can make ourselves righteous. Jesus said they appeared righteous on the outside, but on the inside were "full of hypocrisy and wickedness" (Matthew 23:28). Instead of submitting to the righteousness that comes from God, they sought to establish their own.

Now let's jump back to Revelation 3.

The traditional view is that the Laodiceans were complacent and lackadaisical, but I suspect they were as zealous as Pharisees. Their religious activity was well known. Jesus said, "I know your deeds." What were the Laodiceans doing? It doesn't really matter, but we do know Jesus was not impressed.

> You say, "I am rich; I have acquired wealth and do not need a thing." But you do not realize that you are wretched, pitiful, poor, blind and naked. (Revelation 3:17)

The Laodiceans were full of religious pride. Like the Pharisees, their attitude was, "We've got it made and don't need anything from anyone." Instead of being silenced by the law, they were boastful and self-assured. Instead of acknowledging the poverty of their empty lives, they bragged about their self-sufficiency.

Jesus went to the cross so that we might be liberated from sin and redeemed from the condemnation of the law. To respond with an attitude that says, "I need nothing" is to insult the Spirit of grace and trample the Son of God underfoot. It's to stand with the Pharisees in smug self-righteousness and brag of how much you are doing for God.

Jesus surely loved the Laodiceans, but he found their religion hard to swallow. It's not hard to see why. What could be more nauseating to Jesus than the attitude that says, "You died for nothing."

Who's wretched and poor?

Now we begin to understand why Jesus called the Laodiceans "wretched, pitiful, poor, blind and naked." If they had lived under the law, they would've known this already, for the law reveals our poverty and shame. Paul looked into the mirror of the law and said, "What a wretched man I am" (Romans 7:24). Even without the law they should've known this from their own guilty consciences. But the lukewarm Laodiceans didn't know they were wretched, so Jesus had to tell them. It's not that Jesus is in the condemning business, but you will never appreciate the grace of God if you don't see your need for it.

And this is why manmade religion is so dangerous. Nothing will keep you out of the kingdom of heaven like the lie that says, "I can make myself good enough for God." And nothing will keep you from the grace of God like the faithless quest for self-improvement. Sin will kill you, but religion will inoculate you against the only cure.

Who's wretched and pitiful? It's the one living in the pigpen of self-sufficiency. Who's poor? It is the one who rejects the riches of God's grace. Who's blind? It is the one who does not see what Jesus has done for him. Who's naked? It is the one clothed with filthy acts of self-righteousness.

There are those who say, "I am rich and do not need a thing" and those who say, "I am poor and have a great many needs." Only the latter can be saved, and in Christ they are saved to the uttermost.

How do we "buy" our salvation?

I said at the start that Jesus has wonderful words for us, and here they are:

> I counsel you to buy from me gold refined in the fire, so you can become rich; and white clothes to wear, so you can cover your shameful nakedness; and salve to put on your eyes, so you can see. (Revelation 3:18)

Is Jesus saying salvation is something that can be bought? And if the Laodiceans were truly poor, how could they afford to buy anything?

To buy something is to exchange something we own for something else. Jesus is counseling the Laodiceans to give up what they have (wretched poverty) in exchange for three things: refined gold, which speaks of Christ our everlasting treasure; white clothes, which refer to his perfect righteousness; and salve, which is a revelation of his perfect work.

The new life Jesus offers is free, but we still have to buy into it. You might say we buy salvation by exchanging our sins for his forgiveness, but the real exchange is his life for ours. Jesus took our broken lives and gave us his abundant life. He took our hurts and gave us his healing. He took our death and gave us his life.

No doubt there will be some who worry that I am painting an overly rosy picture of salvation. They will frown because I'm not preaching a more balanced message of sacrifice and personal responsibility. They want you to know that there is a cost to following Jesus, and they are right. The cost is your life. You cannot call him Lord without handing over your crown.

But see the bigger picture. See what you get in return! This is hardly a fair deal. God favors us with this exchange. We give him our broken, ramshackle little lives and in return get him and everything besides. This is the scandal of the new covenant. This is the good news for the poor and the deal of a lifetime.[1]

If salvation means nothing more to you than self-denial and personal sacrifice, you're missing the benefits of grace. Without him we are poor, naked, and blind. With him we're truly and eternally blessed. Jesus encouraged the Laodiceans to buy from him "so you can become rich." When you have Jesus, you have the greatest treasure in the universe.

What does Jesus want us to do?

> As many as I love, I rebuke and chasten. Therefore be zealous and repent. (Revelation 3:19, NKJV)

It's easy to dislike religious people. After all, they're guilt-dispensing fault finders. And don't forget it was religious people who put Jesus on the cross. But the amazing thing is Jesus loves religious people. He loves 'em to bits! Think about it. When Jesus came to earth he adopted as his home the most religious nation on the planet. When he departed the earth he did so from its most religious city. And now, sitting in heaven, he's sending love notes to the religious Laodiceans. "Your religion makes me sick, but *you* I love."

> So be enthusiastic and in earnest and burning with zeal and repent. (Revelation 3:19b, AMP)

Jesus speaks in language we understand. The Laodiceans were zealous with a carnal zeal, so Jesus says to them, "You want to be zealous? How about zealously repenting of your unbelief. All that natural fervor and enthusiasm you have for dead works, why not direct that towards something healthy like free grace?"

Jesus is such a good shepherd. There's no guilt-tripping, no brow-beating, just a wonderful exhortation to do that which we wanted to do all along but didn't know how. His gracious words are the cure for lifeless religion.

If there is apathy in the church, perhaps it's because people are tired of hearing they are not doing enough for God. They are weary of being told they are not hot enough, working enough, or shouting "Amen" enough. The remedy is to preach pure, undiluted grace. Let people drink grace straight from the tap, and they will repent from dead works with joy. Genuine enthusiasm comes not from what we have done for God, but from appreciating what he has done for us. And he has done it all.

> Behold, I stand at the door and knock. If anyone hears my voice and opens the door, I will come in to him and dine with him, and he with me. (Revelation 3:20, NKJV)

Have you ever known people who were so smug and arrogant they made you sick? Did you feel like spending time with them? Probably not. Yet here's Jesus asking if he can join them for dinner. He's outside knocking on the door saying, "I want to come in and be with you forever." The love of God is amazing.

What does Jesus want us to do? He wants us to behold him, hear him, and open the door of our hearts to him. Do that and you will benefit from this wonderful promise:

> To him who overcomes I will grant to sit with me on My throne, as I also overcame and sat down with my Father on his throne. (Revelation 3:21, NKJV)

Jesus is not challenging us to a do-or-die obstacle course. He's reminding us that he has overcome the world and that through him so have we (see 1 John 5:4–5).

If you have been ruined by religion, the letter to the Laodiceans is Christ's cure for you. It's his antidote for those poisoned by a toxic cocktail of grace and works. Jesus is not challenging us to impress him with our zeal and hard work. He is exhorting us to repent from dead works and receive him with open hearts.

The good news is not an invitation to get busy for Jesus. Nor is it the threat of expulsion for those Christ has qualified. The good news is the happy revelation that, in him, we are already seated in heavenly places. From that position of rest, we reign with him in life.

9. How Do I Endure to the End?

Can you lose your salvation if you don't endure to the end? There are nearly two dozen scriptures in the New Testament that have some bearing on this question. In this chapter we will look at three of these scriptures. (We will look at more later in the book.) The three scriptures are all quotes from Jesus:

He who endures to the end will be saved. (Matthew 10:22, 24:13; Mark 13:13, NKJV)

At first glance Jesus seems to be saying, "Salvation hangs on your endurance. If you don't endure, you're not fit for the kingdom." If so, this is not good news. You may worry, "What if I don't stand firm to the end? What if I have a bad day, a bad month, or a bad year? What if I stumble?"

What is Jesus saying here? Is he saying life is one big probationary period and only those who perform flawlessly every day will qualify for the kingdom? Well if he were, he would be contradicting promises he made elsewhere (see chapter 16).

Jesus is not talking about eternal salvation, but rather staying alive in the face of persecution. He is describing what can happen to those who preach his gospel of grace. This becomes clear when we compare *what Jesus said would happen* with *what actually happened* in Paul's case (see Table on next page).

Paul was arguably the greatest gospel preacher of the first century. He is famous for planting churches, writing letters, and standing up to those who opposed his message of grace. But what is not so well known is that Paul often fled hostile situations.

In Lystra, Paul was dragged outside the city, stoned, and left for dead (Acts 14:19). The next day he quit the town and went to Derbe.

In Thessalonica and Berea, it was the same story. Trouble started brewing, and Paul left before it got out of hand (Acts 17).

Paul stayed two years in Ephesus and then left after a riot (Acts 20:1). When faced with mortal persecution, Paul typically walked away — he endured and stayed alive.

93

What Jesus said would happen	What happened to Paul
Be on your guard; you will be handed over to the local councils and be flogged in the synagogues (Matthew 10:17).	Paul was flogged by the Jews on five separate occasions (2 Corinthians 11:24).
On my account you will be brought before governors and kings as witnesses to them and to the Gentiles (Matthew 10:18).	Paul was brought before two governors, one king, and a Caesar and witnessed to all of them (Acts 24–26).
But when they arrest you, do not worry about what to say or how to say it (Matthew 10:19).	Paul didn't worry but was happy to speak before these men (Acts 26:2).
At that time you will be given what to say, for it will not be you speaking, but the Spirit of your Father speaking through you (Matthew 10:19–20).	Paul's words to those in authority made it into the Bible, so they must've been inspired.
Brother will betray brother to death … (Matthew 10:21).	Paul's Jewish brothers tried to kill him in Lystra and plotted his murder in Jerusalem (Acts 23); his Roman brothers beat him with rods in Philippi (Acts 16:22).
You will be hated by everyone because of me … (Matthew 10:22).	Paul was hated by all kinds of people — Jews and Gentiles (see above).
… but the one who stands firm to the end will be saved (Matthew 10:22).	Despite intense and mortal opposition, Paul stayed alive.
When you are persecuted in one place, flee to another (Matthew 10:23).	Paul typically left any place he was persecuted (Acts 13:51, 14:20, 16:40, 17:10).

Imagine what might have happened if Paul had stayed in Lystra after being stoned. Imagine if he had thought, *Jesus died for Lystra. I've got to stay and finish the job even if it kills me.* The Jews would've attacked him again and this time really finished him off. But Paul didn't stay. *Plenty of cities in the world.* He moved on to Derbe.

Paul was one of the bravest men in the Bible, but he was no fool. He knew that a dead apostle serves no one and that the best way to keep preaching the gospel is to stay out of trouble. So whenever he encountered life-threatening persecution, he heeded Jesus' words about fleeing to another city and moved on.

The one time that didn't happen was when Paul ignored the warnings of the Holy Spirit and headed directly into trouble in Jerusalem (Acts 21:11). In other words, Paul did the opposite of what Jesus recommended and, as a result, found himself chained and on a boat bound for a Roman prison.

Jesus said if they persecuted him, they would persecute us as well. But while Jesus had to go to the cross and die, we don't have to. His is a finished work. Our deaths add nothing to his. Better to follow Paul's example and live to preach another day than die at the hand of a madman or an unjust state.[1]

Whether you're a believer in China, Iran, or California, it's always a good idea to avoid trouble, endure to the end, and stay safe. There's a time to dig in and a time to run. If people are coming at you with stones and whips, that may be a sign that it's time to get out of Dodge.

Why does the gospel of grace spark hostility?

The gospel of grace elicits strong reactions. Some people love it, others hate it. It never ceases to amaze me that when I tell people God is good and his love for them is greater than their sin, some respond with indignation and wrath. This baffles me. It makes me think I did a poor job conveying the good news. "My apologies, I wasn't clear. Let me try again. God really loves you and he has forgiven all your sins on account of his grace. Isn't that wonderful?" And they tear my head off.

It's not just me. I've seen grace-preaching pastors bullied out of their own pulpits. I've seen ministers disown their grace-loving children. I've seen families split and friendships end over grace. Why? Because grace is threatening to those who have invested their lives in a system that rewards hard work and good behavior.

When you have spent years earning gold stars, the last thing you want to hear is that the stars count for nothing. When you have made a point of avoiding sin and being a faithful churchgoer, you won't be thrilled to learn that those who enjoyed the pleasures of sin for a season are loved just as much as you are. You'll be offended. And if your livelihood depends on the regular giving of those who believe they must give to be blessed, you'll resist any message that says every spiritual blessing is already ours in Christ.

But that's only part of the reason why some are opposed to the "dangerous teaching" of grace. The bigger reason is they see this grace message as offensive to a bookkeeping God. "God sees your sin. Sin must be paid for and you're going to pay, either now, through contrition and discipline, or later, through fire."

So their opposition, which would otherwise be merely personal, becomes ideological, a religious crusade against heretics under the influence of Satan. I know of what I speak. For preaching grace, I have been called a wolf in sheep's clothing, a false teacher, a heretic, and a devil — all on the same day! This is ugly and unjust, but it is a common experience for those who proclaim the good news of God's grace. Jesus said,

> … the time is coming when anyone who kills you will think they are offering a service to God. They will do such things because they have not known the Father or me. (John 16:2b–3)

Religious people persecuted Jesus all the way to the cross and they hounded Paul from one city to another. To this day the religious and powerful continue to oppose the gospel of grace that Jesus revealed and Paul preached.

What is the leaven of the Pharisees?

Jesus said, "Beware of the leaven of the Pharisees, which is hypocrisy" (Luke 12:1, NKJV). Why do we need to be on our guard if others are acting like hypocrites? Because those who have bought into a lie do not always react well to the truth.

The Pharisees claimed to represent God, but their actions revealed they didn't know him. Even when the Son of God came and stood in front of them, they didn't recognize him. And when he told them who he really was, they said he was of the devil and tried to kill him. This happened on numerous occasions, and Jesus typically responded by walking away. He withdrew, moved on, and stayed alive.[2]

> Then the Pharisees went out and began to plot with the Herodians how they might kill Jesus. Jesus withdrew with his disciples to the lake ... (Mark 3:6–7a)

If you dare to walk by grace, you can expect opposition from the Pharisees and Herodians. A Pharisee is a religious hypocrite who treats grace the same way the original Pharisees treated Jesus. He may talk about grace as though he knows something about it, but when grace is revealed he says it's of the devil and then tries to kill it.

The religious hypocrite likes grace but only in moderation. Proclaim radical grace and he will chide you for being unbalanced or extreme. He may warn you to steer clear of what he perceives to be a dangerous teaching. And to him grace is dangerous, for it undermines everything he's worked for. It elevates tax-collectors and sinners to the same exalted status he has attained on his own.

The religious hypocrite accepts grace in theory, just not in practice. He may be willing to let the riff-raff into the kingdom, but it irks him when grace throws parties for prodigals while ignoring his years of faithful service. The hypocrite feels he must resist radical grace, for it threatens to tear down the walls of reputation and ministry that separate the elite from the rest.

Some will say, "Grace is for sinners," by which they mean grace is *only* for sinners. Grace is not for them. "We are saved by grace but sanctified through hard work and discipline."

Or they will say, "Grace is an important doctrine," meaning grace needs to be balanced with other important doctrines like holiness and submission. "Grace is a good idea, but you will not experience it unless you first walk in obedience."

We need to be wary of lines like these, for they lead to hypocrisy. Those who say such things treat grace as little more than grease for the gears of your self-effort. They don't understand that grace is the whole engine, the gearbox, and everything else. Apart from grace, we can do nothing. Zip. Nada.

Live confidently under grace and you can expect trouble from the Pharisee. Resist his manipulation and he will condemn you in the name of the Lord. He will seek to skewer you with scriptures and silence you with warnings. He may even try to assassinate your character. And while he is doing all of this he will be telling himself that he is doing the Lord's work and protecting the church.

What is the leaven of the Herod?

Jesus said, "Beware of the leaven of the Pharisees and the leaven of Herod" (Mark 8:15, NKJV). A Herod is a self-made king who treats grace the same way the original Herod treated Jesus—by trying to kill him (see Matthew 2:13).

The Herods of the world—the bosses, rulers, and power-brokers—have no time for grace because their world runs on the principles of *un*grace. These principles are well known: "The early bird gets the worm." "No pain, no gain." "There is no such thing as a free lunch." "Demand your rights." "Get what you pay for."[3]

The leaven of Herod is the belief that success is for the self-made man. Rewards come to those who earn them, and everyone gets what they deserve.

In Herod's world everyone knows their place and everyone has their price. Those at the bottom work so that those at the top can enjoy the good life. The good news according to Herod is, "Play by the rules and you may rise from your lowly station. Work hard, don't make trouble, and maybe one day you will get a bigger stake in the game."

But King Jesus offers us a better gospel. In his kingdom your worth is not determined by your productivity, but your Father's love. King Herod says, "You are mine. You work for me." But grace proclaims, "You are a child of the Most High and a slave of no man."

The rich and powerful are opposed to grace because it threatens to empty the slave markets on which their empires are built. "Grace is bad business," they say. "We have to stop this thing before it spreads." It was this grace-killing mindset that Paul encountered in Ephesus.

In many of the towns he visited, Paul was met with religious opposition, but Ephesus was different. In Ephesus it was the merchants and craftsmen who opposed his gospel (see Acts 19). They were worried about their trade in idols. To protect their business interests they instigated a riot and seized two of Paul's traveling companions.

As demonstrated in Ephesus, Herod cannot tolerate grace because it weakens his hold over others. For Herod to remain on the throne, he has to keep you under his thumb. His dog-eat-dog world requires a steady supply of fresh dogs. Consequently, the Herods in your life—your employers and those with power and prestige—will never encourage you in your grace journey. They will pressure you to perform, climb the ladder, and stay in their game.

Follow after grace and you may find yourself in a tug of war between two kings. King Jesus will be gently drawing you towards ever-increasing freedom, while King Herod will seek to keep you bound with cords of stress, ambition, and insecurity.

A pattern I have often seen is this: Someone hears the gospel of grace and gets a whiff of the free air of heaven. They may have been beaten down by debt and circumstance, but when grace comes along they respond with joy. "Thank God almighty, I am free at last." But before they are out of the prison door, something happens in their job and they are sucked right back down under the weight of manmade expectations. New cares and worries emerge to keep the gospel from bearing fruit in their lives. They get seduced from the truth of Jesus by Herod's lies.

Live for grace and you will find yourself in conflict with modern-day Pharisees and Herods. They are not your enemy, but since the principles they stand on are fundamentally opposed to grace, they will create trouble for you. The temptation will be to respond in the flesh, but doing so will only lead to more trouble. A wiser response may be to withdraw like Jesus or walk away like Paul.

Life is too short to live in reaction to the angry opposition of grace-haters. Sheep and wolves never get along. So "be as shrewd as snakes and as innocent as doves" (Matthew 10:16).

How do we live at peace in a hostile world?

Our world is marred by violence, greed, and all the fruits of sin. What this world desperately needs is a revelation of Jesus and his peaceable kingdom. But how do we live at peace in a world of hostile Herods and Pharisees?

Jesus said, "When you go someplace to reveal the good news of heaven, let your peace rest on that place" (see Matthew 10:12). This seems an odd thing to say, but it makes perfect sense if you grew up watching *Star Trek*. In the *Star Trek* universe, visitors from faraway places would arrive with unknown intentions. If they said, "We come in peace," you knew all would be well. Their intentions were peaceable.

That's how it is with us. Wherever we go, we go in peace. We don't come swinging swords or firing photon torpedoes. We have no interest in picking sides or partisan politics. Instead, we are presenting a radical alternative to anything this world offers, namely, a message of hope from another kingdom.

If it is possible, as far as it depends on you, live at peace with everyone. (Romans 12:18)

For too long Christianity has been associated with the unfortunate image of the bloodied crusader. But the true sons of God are peacemakers (Matthew 5:9). Our aim is to live at peace with everyone. When that's not possible, then it may be time to move on, change the subject, change the conversation, perhaps even change towns (see Matthew 10:14).

I occasionally get messages like this:

Paul, I've come to realize that God really loves me and he's forgiven all my sins. I was so excited to share this at church, but the pastor stood up afterwards and shot me down. He said I was presenting an unbalanced version of grace. Later he sent me a message saying I wasn't to speak about grace again. What's going on?

What's going on is a wedge of truth is beginning to divide "father from son and mother from daughter." It's not pleasant, but it happens. Those who have seen grace can't unsee it, and those who haven't can't relate.

What can you do in such a situation? You have two options: Stop talking about grace or start a new conversation someplace else. The temptation will be to engage in debate, but little good will come of it. A wiser approach is to ask the Holy Spirit, "How can I reveal the peace of heaven in this situation?" This is what distinguishes the sons of God from others — we make peace where they make war.

To recap, "Endure to the end and be saved" is not the bad news of conditional salvation. Jesus is simply saying you cannot fulfill the Great Commission if you're dead or otherwise silenced. If you are being persecuted for preaching the gospel in Lystra, move to Derbe. "When you are persecuted in one place, flee to another" (Matthew 10:23).

The gospel of peace is not proclaimed by waging religious wars. No one ever got saved through an argument. The last thing an angry and violent world needs is angry and violent Christians. What this world desperately needs is a revelation of the Prince of peace by those who have embraced his gospel of peace.

10. Who Can Take Communion?

As the communion plate came closer and closer, I was filled with terror. Condemnation was just minutes away. Why was I afraid? I had unresolved sin in my life. I was ten years old and I had argued with my sister before church. I knew those who took communion in an unworthy manner risked judgment, possibly even death, for the Bible told me so:

> So then, whoever eats the bread or drinks the cup of the Lord in an unworthy manner will be guilty of sinning against the body and blood of the Lord ... Those who eat and drink without discerning the body of Christ eat and drink judgment on themselves. That is why many among you are weak and sick, and a number of you have fallen asleep. (1 Corinthians 11:27–30)

Thankfully, I was wrong.

The passage above must be one of the most misunderstood passages in the Bible. It is regularly used to deny communion to those who need it and it is frightening to ten-year-olds. But as we will see, it is one of the most liberating scriptures in the Bible.

What's the big deal with communion?

> The Lord Jesus, on the night he was betrayed, took bread, and when he had given thanks, he broke it and said, "This is my body, which is for you; do this in remembrance of me." In the same way, after supper he took the cup, saying, "This cup is the new covenant in my blood; do this, whenever you drink it, in remembrance of me." (1 Corinthians 11:23b–25)

Communion is pretty simple. It's just bread and wine, or flatbread and grape juice, or whatever you have on hand. The significance of communion — or the Lord's Supper or the Eucharist or the breaking of bread or whatever you prefer to call it — is not what you eat and drink, but why you do it. Jesus said, "Do this in remembrance of me." Communion is about him, not us. If you are focused on yourself during communion, you're doing it wrong. Communion is not a time for examining yourself for sin. It's a time for remembering Jesus.

But what aspect of Jesus are we to remember? Paul tells us:

> For whenever you eat this bread and drink this cup, you proclaim the Lord's death until he comes. (1 Corinthians 11:26)

Jesus did many good things, but ultimately he came to die so that we might live. We proclaim, not mourn, the Lord's death by giving thanks. Indeed, this is what the word *Eucharist* literally means; giving thanks. Communion is not a time for confessing sins, but for saying, "Thank you, Jesus."[1]

What is the significance of the bread? It represents Jesus, the bread of life that came down from heaven to give life to the world (John 6:48, 51). Eating the communion bread is an opportunity to say, "Thank you, Lord, for your body that was pierced and broken so that I might truly live."

What is the significance of the cup? The cup represents the most precious commodity in the universe, namely the blood of Jesus that underwrites the new covenant:

> Then he took a cup, and when he had given thanks, he gave it to them, saying, "Drink from it, all of you. This is my blood of the covenant, which is poured out for many for the forgiveness of sins." (Matthew 26:27–28)

Drinking from the communion cup is an opportunity to say, "Thank you, Lord, for your blood that cleanses me from all sin and makes me white as snow."

Without the blood, the gospel is no gospel and the cross is nothing more than two beams of wood. As the hymnist Robert Lowry wrote, we stand on "nothing but the blood of Jesus." Our cleansing, our wholeness, our pardon, our hope, our peace, our righteousness, our overcoming are all possible because Jesus bled and died. This is what we remember when we take communion. This is the good news in a cup!

How do we take communion in an unworthy manner?

Proclaiming the Lord's death ought to be an occasion of joy and celebration. Was there ever a better reason to party than this? We who were enslaved by sin are now free. We who were dead now live.

Yet for many, communion is not a time of celebration. It's a time of anxious introspection and fear. This is partly because of what Paul says next:

So then, whoever eats the bread or drinks the cup of the Lord in an unworthy manner will be guilty of sinning against the body and blood of the Lord. (1 Corinthians 11:27)

My ten-year-old self panicked because I thought I was about to take communion in an unworthy manner. I wasn't worthy because there was sin in my life. I knew this because my conscience was pounding on me like Mike Tyson.

Jesus said, "Eat and drink in remembrance of me," but I was too busy remembering myself. I was self-conscious instead of Christ-conscious. *If only I had had time to make amends,* I thought. *If only I had cleansed myself before coming to church.* This is the mindset of DIY religion.

It is the nature of the flesh to try and fix things. We break it, we buy it. We sin, we repent. "There, now all is mended. I don't need God, I fixed it myself." Beware these fig leaves!

We are sometimes told to examine ourselves for sin before we take communion, as though our sins disqualified us from coming to the table. But Jesus died for sinners. He died for the lost and the least, the damaged and the hurting. He died for the worst of us and for those who fight on the way to church.

If you think you need to clean yourself before coming to Jesus, you are living under a lie. If you think the Lord's table requires minimum standards of worthiness, you have missed the cross. If you are tempted to hide like Adam whenever God appears, you need to hear the good news of his grace.

DIY religion says, "Here are some fig leaves of confession and repentance – get busy sewing." But grace says, "Come as you are and let the blood of Jesus deal with your sins and guilty conscience." DIY religion would have you run and hide. But grace draws you to the table of grace to receive mercy and find grace in your hour of need.

> Everyone ought to examine themselves before they eat of the bread and drink from the cup. (1 Corinthians 11:28)

The word for examine means "to test and by implication approve."[2] Paul is not saying, "Better make sure you're a real Christian. Better check and see if there isn't some disqualifying sin in you." It doesn't work like that. In the old covenant, the high priest examined the sacrificial lamb, not the one who brought it. In the new covenant, Christ is your Lamb without blemish or defect (1 Peter 1:19). Examine *him*. See yourself as tested and approved *in him*.

Communion is not a time for sin examination but Jesus examination. The next time your conscience tries to condemn you as unworthy, remind yourself that Christ died for the unworthy. Tell yourself, "In Christ, I am righteous and holy. I am not justified because of what I did, but because of what *he* did. On the cross he did away with my sins once and for all, and through his precious blood I have been eternally forgiven."

Taking communion in a worthy manner does not mean coming to the table dressed in your best fig leaves. It is marveling at the cross with humble adoration. It's saying, "Thank you, Jesus, for dying so that I might live."

Who is guilty of the body and blood?

The Corinthians did communion so badly that 2,000 years later, we're still talking about it. But what exactly were they doing wrong? They were eating like pigs, getting drunk, and humiliating those too poor to bring food to share (see 1 Corinthians 11:21–22).

The Corinthians were certainly disgraceful in their conduct, but were they "guilty of sinning against the body and blood of the Lord," as Paul suggests in verse 27? If so, this would be a serious

106

charge, for the word *guilty* is applied to the saints nowhere else in the Bible. In Christ, you have been judged not guilty for all time.

Paul is not condemning Christians. Nor is he accusing the saints in Corinth of being guilty sinners. He is simply saying, "Communion is a big deal. We know this because of what happens to those who reject Christ's death."

The cross of Christ is the great divider of humanity. It's not that Jesus separates those he loves from those he hates, for he loves the whole world. But people separate themselves by their response to his sacrificial love.

Jesus' death offends some people. They don't see the grace in it. To be guilty of the body and blood is to hear the good news of the cross and dismiss it as irrelevant. It's saying, "I don't need Jesus. His death means nothing to me."

Were the Corinthians saying this? No. No Christian ever would. Paul mentions it to say this: because Christ's death is a big deal, communion is a big deal. You wouldn't get drunk and act like a pig at Calvary, so why do it at communion?

What does it mean to drink judgment on myself?

For those who eat and drink without discerning the body of Christ eat and drink judgment on themselves. (1 Corinthians 11:29)

The word for judgment in this passage almost always means a negative judgment. The King James Bible translates it as "drinking damnation." In other words, to come to the Lord's table with a stubborn and unbelieving heart is bad. It's voting against Christ. It's saying, "I don't need grace."

There are two things you need to understand about this judgment verse. First, Paul is not describing believers. As a Christian you may act like an unbeliever — the Corinthians certainly did — but you are not defined by what you do. You are defined by Jesus. By definition, a Christian can no more eat and drink judgment on himself than he can blaspheme the Holy Spirit. It's simply not possible.

Second, the judgment Paul describes is self-inflicted. God is not reaching down from heaven and smiting the scornful with the damnation stamp. They are damning themselves.

Think of Judas, who knew Jesus as well as the other disciples, but unlike them, never saw him as Lord. At the Last Supper Judas ate the bread and drank the cup, but since his heart was full of unbelief these symbols meant nothing to him. By closing his eyes to the truth of Christ and siding with the blind Pharisees, Judas condemned himself. After several years of witnessing the grace of God in action, the Last Supper was literally his final opportunity to acknowledge Christ. He didn't, and Jesus immediately pronounced the woe that he had brought on his own head (see Luke 22:22).

Someone who has never heard the gospel may yet receive it. But those who have heard and hardened their hearts to the good news are guilty of the blood and body of Jesus. By taking communion they remove any claim to ignorance. They can no longer say, "I didn't know Jesus died for me," because they are eating and drinking in commemoration of that very death.

To partake of communion unworthily is to be unmoved by the death of God's Son. It is to remain ungrateful for the greatest act of love you will ever know. Shutting your eyes to the love of Christ and following Judas out the door is fatal. Although judgment day still awaits you, you have essentially brought judgment on yourself ahead of schedule. This is what it means to drink judgment on yourself. It's saying, "I choose to stand with Judas and the Pharisees." In doing so you are standing with the condemned.

And this leads us to a very important question.

Who can take communion?

"And now as we turn to the communion table, I would like to invite all who love Jesus and call him 'Lord' to join with us in partaking of the elements. If you're visiting with us today and you don't know Jesus, feel free to spend this time in quiet reflection. Communion is something that Christians do to remember Jesus' death."

How I wish I could take those words back! Could I not see the staggering ungraciousness of my remarks? Was I blind to the unholy line I was drawing between Us (welcome to take communion) and Them (not welcome)? Jesus died for all, but all were not being invited to remember his death. Grace is inclusive, but as a young pastor I made communion exclusive.

I was not alone. Many churches have rules stipulating who can and cannot break bread. Some say it's inappropriate for unbelievers to participate and make a point of "inviting" them not to do so. Since unbelievers don't value the cross, the thinking goes, they shouldn't be allowed to drink judgment on themselves by taking communion.

But don't you find it interesting that Paul, despite all his warnings about "drinking judgment," never says this? He never says, "Make sure unbelievers don't take communion." Instead, he says a man ought to examine himself before taking communion (1 Corinthians 11:28).

Since there is a possibility of taking communion in an unworthy fashion (meaning with unbelief in the finished work of the cross), and since by doing so we are effectively drinking damnation on ourselves (meaning we are refusing the grace that saves us), an opportunity should be given for self-examination. And what is the proper way to examine ourselves? Answer: in light of the cross.

We have already seen that Christians who examine themselves do so *in Christ*. In him you are as righteous and holy as he is. But what about an unbeliever? What about those who have never given thanks for grace? This is their chance! Communion is their opportunity to take a moment and consider all God has done for them. Deny them communion and you deny their opportunity. You're basically saying, "Don't respond to the gospel."

Somehow Paul's words in 1 Corinthians 11 have been twisted into a worthiness test for communion. "Examine yourself before you eat and drink" is often interpreted as "look inside for sin, and if there is any, don't partake." I know some churches even go so far as to stipulate minimum standards of worthiness. They say you must be a believer or a baptized believer or voting member of the church before you can break bread.

It's like there's this Christian caste system and at the bottom are the filthy, untouchable sinners who definitely shouldn't break bread because anyone who rejects Jesus is obviously unworthy. That's basically what I was saying in my church. By telling visitors (they might be sinners—who let them in here?) that they were "free" not to partake of communion, I was sending the message, "This is not for you. You're not good enough for Jesus." I was implicitly judging them as unworthy of the body and blood. Of course I didn't think of it in such terms. I thought I was honoring Jesus and protecting sinners from judgment. Slowly it began to dawn on me that there was something odd about denying communion to sinners. After all, didn't Jesus die for sinners?

Paul is not prescribing worthiness tests for communion. He is saying "Jesus' death is a big deal, so take a moment to reflect on it. If Jesus' death means something to you, then communion is a time to savor and celebrate. But if the significance of his death is news to you, here's your chance to process it. Here's an opportunity to repent and believe the good news."

For if we would judge ourselves, we would not be judged. (1 Corinthians 11:31, NKJV)

Everyone has their day of judgment, but for the Christian, judgment day is in the past. The Christian has looked into the mirror of the law or listened to the accusations of his own conscience, judged himself wanting, and taken hold of the free grace that Jesus provides. His judgment day is thus his salvation day. But for the one who refuses grace and continues to stand on his own merits, judgment day remains in the future. If he continues to scorn grace, his judgment day will be a day of condemnation.

Nevertheless, when we are judged in this way by the Lord, we are being disciplined so that we will not be finally condemned with the world. (1 Corinthians 11:32)

The old world order of sin and death has been condemned. It has no future. A new order based on grace and forgiveness is springing up. Jesus stands astride the old and the new, rescuing all who would abandon the sinking ship. Whoever takes his outreached hand is not condemned, but whoever refuses him is doomed to go down (see John 3:18).

This isn't about signing up for church or getting the right answers on a belief exam. This is about Jesus and what you will do with him. He has done it all. The gift has been given. Our part is simply to take it by faith.

Can unbelievers take communion?

Should unbelievers be excluded from communion? Paul would have found this question preposterous. It's like asking, "Should unbelievers be excluded from the gospel?" Communion is proclaiming the Lord's death. Since the cross is at the heart of the gospel, every time we do communion we are proclaiming the good news.

Is not the cup of thanksgiving for which we give thanks a participation in the blood of Christ? And is not the bread that we break a participation in the body of Christ? (1 Corinthians 10:16)

Isn't the whole point of the gospel to get people to participate in the kingdom of God? Isn't it about inviting them in? So why are we shutting them out during communion?

"But Paul, these sinners don't believe in Jesus." Neither did you once upon a time. But someone showed you grace and you responded with gratitude. Denying communion is denying grace. It's something Jesus never did. Even Judas got communion.

In the old covenant, sinners and the unclean were kept at a distance lest they contaminate the righteous. But Jesus was a friend of sinners. He went into their houses and broke bread with them. He met with thieves, adulterers, and murderers and "contaminated" them with his righteousness. Sinners were radically changed by his awesome grace.

By saying "Communion is only for the worthy," we have turned a new covenant blessing into an old covenant curse and denied grace to those who need it most. Religion draws lines between Us and Them, but grace tears down dividing walls. Nowhere in the Bible will you find any hint of a suggestion that we should exclude people from communion. This is a death-dealing tradition of self-righteous men.

I used to say that communion was for Us but not for Them. In doing so I was acting contrary to the Spirit of grace. But I repented. I changed my tune and began saying, "All are welcome at the Lord's table." I then watched amazed as the Holy Spirit began to reveal the love and grace of God to those who didn't know him.

How should we do communion?

So then, my brothers and sisters, when you gather to eat, you should all eat together. Anyone who is hungry should eat something at home, so that when you meet together it may not result in judgment. And when I come I will give further directions. (1 Corinthians 11:33–34)

Communion at the Corinthian church was a total fiasco. Paul said their meetings did more harm than good (1 Corinthians 11:17). He said this because their table manners made them a disgraceful advertisement for the gospel. "When you come together, it is not the Lord's Supper you eat" (1 Corinthians 11:20). Indeed, it was not. It was the potluck dinner from hell.

Paul wrote to correct their poor behavior. He reminded them of the significance of communion before giving them some practical instructions. He then finished by expressing his hope that their meetings "may not result in judgment." What is this judgment Paul is speaking of? It is the same judgment of verse 29. It's the self-inflicted condemnation of unbelief. When you do communion so badly that it's no longer communion, you impede the gospel, and people suffer for it.

Imagine you had never heard of Jesus and you visited the Corinthian church. You see these followers of Christ getting drunk, hogging the food, and embarrassing those who hadn't brought any. What impression would you leave with? You may think, "These Christians are a joke. I want nothing to do with them and their Christ." Or you may say, "Pass the amphora. I like this drunken Jesus a lot!" Either way, you're going to get the wrong picture of Jesus.

As Christians, our job is to reveal the Jesus who died and rose again. To the degree to which we reveal another Jesus, perhaps a drunken Jesus or a Jesus more concerned with behavior than love, we promote a terminal status quo.

Jesus said, "Preach the gospel of the kingdom." It's the good news of another world for the inhabitants of a condemned one. It's the declaration that death no longer has the last word from One who died and rose again.

Whenever we meet, we have an opportunity to release either the grace of a risen King or the condemnation of a fallen order. We will dispense either the flavor of heaven or the swill of a corrupt world. In acting like pigs, the Corinthians were doing the latter. They were snatching food instead of giving thanks. They were humiliating others instead of giving grace.

If the Corinthians show us how *not* to do communion, then the Jerusalem Christians show us how to do it right:

> They devoted themselves to the apostles' teaching and to fellowship, to the breaking of bread and to prayer. Everyone was filled with awe at the many wonders and signs performed by the apostles. All the believers were together and had everything in common ... They broke bread in their homes and ate together with glad and sincere hearts, praising God and enjoying the favor of all the people. And the Lord added to their number daily those who were being saved. (Acts 2:42–47)

When we reveal the real Jesus at the table of grace, good things happen. Those outside are drawn in, the sick and poor have their needs met, and the result is praise and thanksgiving to God. What does communion look like when it is done well? It looks like heaven.

11. How Does God Deal with Us When We Sin?

My three-year-old son is a regular Michelangelo. The other day he drew a purple-crayon masterpiece on the walls of his bedroom. Needless to say, I was furious. I told him he was a vandal and I belted him within an inch of his life. Then I said if he did it again I'd kick him out of the family.

Of course I did no such thing! And yet this sort of over-the-top reaction is exactly how some imagine their heavenly Father responding when they sin. They say things like, "God convicted me with guilt and then he chastised me with scourging." Or, "God is disciplining me with sickness because I've done terrible things."

This kind of religious talk is based on chopped-up bits of the Bible but is completely uninformed by the gospel of Jesus. It will cause you to look inward instead of upward and to focus on your faults instead of his perfections. It will make you sin-conscious instead of Son-conscious.

For thousands of years manmade religion has preached against sin, and what has it gotten us? More sin. "The fault is you," cries religion. "You are not keeping the rules." So we try harder and fail bigger.

If you have struggled to overcome sin and made a purple-crayon mess of your life, understand that the problem is not your lack of effort. The real culprit is religion that promotes confidence in the flesh over faith in Jesus.

Does God make us feel guilty?

Did Jesus sneak out of heaven against his Father's wishes to come and die for our sins? Of course not. Yet many seem to think that God the Son and God the Father are playing a good cop-bad cop routine with humanity. God the Father is angry with us on account of our sin, but Jesus stands between us, protecting us from his Father's wrath.

I hope you can see how ridiculous this picture is. The Father and the Son do not have different agendas. They are united in heart, both full of grace and truth.

But what about the Holy Spirit? Where does he fit in this picture? According to some, the Holy Spirit is the sheriff of heaven, convicting us of our sins and making us feel guilty:

> But I tell you the truth: It is for your good that I am going away. Unless I go away, the Counselor will not come to you; but if I go, I will send him to you. When he comes, he will convict the world of guilt in regard to sin ... (John 16:7–8, NIV1984)

This is probably the number one teaching on sin in the church: When you sin, the Holy Spirit will convict you of your guilt in regard to your sin. But there's a problem. How can the Holy Spirit convict you of sins he chooses not to remember?

> The Holy Spirit also testifies to us about this... "Their sins and lawless acts I will remember no more." (Hebrews 10:15, 17)

Under the law-keeping covenant, you had to keep track of and account for every single sin. But the covenant of God's grace is characterized by divine forgetfulness:

> For I will forgive their wickedness and will remember their sins no more. (Jeremiah 31:34c)

Why does God choose to forget our sins? Has he gone soft on sin? Quite the contrary. On the cross God gave sin such a smack-down that it will never get back up again. In honor of his complete and total victory over sin, God can now dismiss sin as irrelevant to his eternal purposes in Christ Jesus.

In choosing not to remember sin, God is saying, "I have met the enemy, I have overcome the enemy, and I will not honor the memory of my enemy." Your old master sin has been thoroughly defeated. He's history.

So why does the Bible say God convicts us of *guilt* in regard to sin? It doesn't. If your Bible says he does, chances are you have an old edition of the New International Version. The word *guilt* was added to that Bible in the 1970s by translators working for the New York Bible Society.[1] But the fact is Jesus never said it, and the Holy Spirit doesn't do it. He doesn't need to. We already know we're guilty. Our consciences hammer us with guilt every time we do something wrong. Guilt is a signal that our lives have been disrupted by sin. It's a sign that a hurt needs to be healed.

The problem is we try to fix the hurt with dead religion. We take our sins and hurts to Dr. Law and he gives us bad medicine. He says, "You are not good enough, you are not doing enough, and you need to try harder." We swallow his medicine, but the tumor of guilt gets bigger.

So we go for a second opinion. We visit Dr. Mixture and he says, "You're forgiven, as long as you don't sin. God is so kind he will cleanse you from every sin that you confess." Now we are not only guilty, we are anxious. *What if I miss one sin? Will God be kind then?*

With muddled messages like these, is it any wonder that religious people are among the most neurotic people on the planet?

You need to understand that God is not the one making you feel guilty. God removes guilt; he doesn't give it. To be guilty means to be held responsible for your sin, and God doesn't hold you responsible. Look to the cross, where Jesus took responsibility for all our sin. He bore our sin so that we might bear his righteousness. Under law, the best of us is charged guilty on account of sin. But under grace, the worst of us is charged righteous on account of Jesus.

You may say, "I know I am righteous and justified, yet I still feel guilty." Connect the dots. If you are righteous and justified you cannot be guilty. In Christ you have been judged and found not guilty for all time.

That feeling of guilt is a symptom of unbelief in the goodness of God. Don't let that feeling run around like a rat in the attic. Take it to Jesus and let him deal with it. Do you believe that his blood is God's cure for sin? Then believe it is also his cure for guilt.

Let us draw near to God with a sincere heart and with the full assurance that faith brings, having our hearts sprinkled to cleanse us from a guilty conscience and having our bodies washed with pure water. (Hebrews 10:22)

Recently, someone tried to convince me that God makes us feel guilty for a season in order to bring about his righteous purposes. He said the Holy Spirit uses godly guilt to lead us to repentance. That sounds like religious double-talk to me. The phrase "godly guilt" makes as much sense as "demonic grace." The Holy Spirit and guilt go together like the devil and love. He's the Spirit of grace, not the spirit of guilt.

Guilt is the language of manmade religion, but it's not a language they speak in heaven. You are a citizen of a heavenly kingdom, so speak like it. When sin points an accusing finger at you and shouts "Guilty!" point to the cross and shout back louder, "Forgiven!"

Jesus did not sneak out of heaven on a secret mercy mission, and God did not have a change of heart after the cross. Your heavenly Father is not a guilt-dispenser. Neither is the Holy Spirit.

How does the Holy Spirit convict us?

"I know I've sinned because my conscience has been pricked and I feel bad for what I did. This is evidence of the Holy Spirit's conviction." No it's not. It's evidence of a conscience.

The Holy Spirit will never condemn you or pile guilt on your head because if he did, it would be an admission of defeat. It would be tantamount to saying Christ's work on the cross was an insufficient remedy for your sin.

As an expression of his love and mercy, the Holy Spirit seeks to convict or convince us that Jesus is the cure for sin.

And when he has come, he will convict the world of sin ... because they do not believe in me. (John 16:8–9, NKJV)

It's not that the Holy Spirit convicts the world of the sin of unbelief. Rather, his purpose is to get you to believe Jesus has taken away your sin. "Concerning sin — see Jesus. Believe in him."

"But Paul, I've got some serious sin." That may be, but God has some serious grace, and his serious grace is greater than your serious sin.

It's really very simple. Either Jesus' one-time sacrifice was the cure for the world's sin or it wasn't. If it was, there is nothing you can do to improve upon it. If it wasn't, there is nothing you can do to complete it. Either way, there is nothing you can do.

Why do we get so confused about this? I think part of the reason has to do with the word *convict*. In English, to convict someone is to declare them guilty of an offense. First you are *convicted*, then you become a *convict*. But this is not what the Holy Spirit does. He doesn't fill prisons; he empties them.

I used to do prison ministry. If I told the inmates that the Holy Spirit convicted me of sin, they would think, "He busted you. You were caught red-handed, you bad sinner." What a slanderous portrayal of the Holy Spirit's life-giving ministry. I would have given the impression that he is like the law—or worse, the Accuser. The Holy Spirit is nothing like that.

So what does it mean to say the Holy Spirit convicts us? The original word means to expose or bring into the light. The Holy Spirit convicts us by turning on the lights. He does this not to shame you, but to show you the way to life.[2]

We need a new covenant definition of conviction, one that is not based on our sin and guilt. The Holy Spirit's conviction has nothing to do with your sin and everything to do with God's grace. It's not about the bad thing you've done but the good thing he wants to do in you right now.

Do you remember the woman caught in adultery? Now there's a guilty sinner, lost and without hope. The facts denounce her, the law condemns her, and angry religious men with stones are lining up to dispense a little Old Testament punishment on her head. For this sinner, death is just moments away.

But Jesus intervenes. He stoops to write in the sand, drawing attention from the sinner to himself. Amazingly, all her accusers walk away.

Jesus straightened up and asked her, "Woman—where are they? Has no one condemned you?" "No one, sir," she said.

"Then neither do I condemn you," Jesus declared. "Go now and leave your life of sin." (John 8:10–11)

This is what true conviction looks like. It's Jesus drawing your attention to the radiant light of his love and acceptance. It's the hand of grace lifting your head and shielding you from the heavy stones of condemnation. It's the Son of God speaking in your defense and silencing your accusers.

Religion says, "You'd better stop sinning or God will condemn you." But grace says, "I don't condemn you; I am for you, and I will help you leave your life of sin." This good news is hard to believe. You probably wouldn't be able to receive it, except the Holy Spirit has turned on the lights and convinced you that Jesus is faithful and true.

When you sin, your conscience may condemn you, the law may condemn you, and the Spanish Inquisition may condemn you. But while all of this condemning is going on, the Holy Spirit will be there to remind you of your righteousness in Christ Jesus. *This is what empowers us to sin no more.* Not the unsurprising discovery that we messed up, but the outrageously good news that God justifies sinners.

How does God deal with us when we sin?

"When you sin, you offend a holy and righteous God. You incur his displeasure and anger. So examine your heart and confess your trespasses to God so he can forgive you." Statements like these reveal a great confusion about the finished work of the cross. They completely miss the heart of our Father, who loves us regardless of our behavior.

Does God care when we sin? Of course he does. What parent doesn't? But he doesn't whip out his video camera and record your mistakes as evidence to be used against you. Nor does he put a black mark next to your name. Love keeps no record of wrongs (1 Corinthians 13:5). Our sins grieve the Holy Spirit—they make him sad—but he doesn't withdraw, condemn, or guilt-trip us in response. As the psalm-writer said:

11. How does God deal with us when we sin?

He does not treat us as our sins deserve or repay us according to our iniquities. (Psalm 103:10)

We have heard that God is good all the time, and he is. But the gospel goes further than that. The gospel declares that God is good all the time *to you.* Even when you sin, he is still good. He does not treat you as your sins deserve but continues to pour out his love upon you. Your sins have more chance of dimming the sun than diminishing your Father's great love for you.

I know this may be hard for you to process. We have been raised to beware sin, to resist sin, to run from sin, to overcome sin. With so much emphasis on sin, guilt, and shame, is it any wonder so many of us are sin-conscious instead of Christ-conscious? We need to be set free from this unhealthy obsession with sin.

I'm not minimizing the dangers of sin. Your mistakes and bad decisions can hurt you and others. I'm saying God does not relate to us on the basis of our behavior. Rather, he deals with us in love.

Those confused by grace worry about what God thinks of them when they sin. "Does God see my sin?" Of course he does. He sees everything. But in the new covenant a better question is, "How does God deal with me when I go astray?" The answer is: gently and with compassion (see Hebrews 5:2). When you stumble and make a hash of your life, your Father doesn't pull out a whip. He responds with affirming love and transforming grace.

Picture your life as a boat sailing across the trackless ocean. You are free to go any direction you like. The problem is there are risks involved. You can't predict the weather, you can't see over the horizon, and you don't know where the hidden reefs are. You need a guide.

Now at this point you may be thinking, "Thank God for the Bible." But the Bible is not your guide book. Although it contains much that is helpful, it was not written to help you navigate life. For that you need a Navigator. As someone once said, "We are not following a manual; we are following Emmanuel."

When he, the Spirit of truth, has come, he will guide you into all truth. (John 16:13a, NKJV)

The Holy Spirit is the guide who leads you into all truth. Since Jesus is the truth, the Holy Spirit will always steer you towards Jesus. This is the primary way in which the Holy Spirit keeps us safe from sin. Let me give you an everyday example of how he does this.

As a father of small children I am regularly stretched beyond my coping abilities. I get tired and frustrated and sometimes I become a bad dad. I grizzle and growl and frighten my children. If you are a parent, you'll know what I'm talking about.

How does the Holy Spirit respond when I act this way? Here's what he doesn't do. He doesn't come and say, "What a lousy father you were today. You are a bad dad." I already know that.

The Holy Spirit doesn't shame me but seeks to guide me to Jesus. And where's Jesus? He's within me like a treasure inside a jar of clay (2 Corinthians 4:7). Because he is in us and with us, we have a choice. We can choose to walk in weary flesh, or we can allow Christ to reveal his grace through us.

How does it happen? For some, grace manifests as an inspiring, mental picture of themselves doing really well. Others may be reminded of a scripture that imparts life into a stressful situation. But for me, the most common experience is I find myself abounding in supernatural love.

This doesn't happen automatically. And it certainly doesn't happen when I am leaning on my own strength and understanding. But if I take a moment to ask my heavenly Father for help, grace comes. A light goes on, and I begin to see my kids as my Father sees me—as precious and dearly loved.

It's hard to explain, but everything changes. Suddenly their noise and energy no longer bother me. I feel bigger. It's like my shoulders grow wider. Instead of being overwhelmed I find myself wanting to stoke the fires of their youthful exuberance just to see what happens next. Do you understand? It's a completely different me. It is Christ revealing his kid-loving character through me, and it's miraculous. I am transformed from bad dad into the best dad in the world.

How does the Holy Spirit deal with us when we fall to pieces? By revealing Jesus and his supernatural grace. The jar of your life may be crumbling, but the treasure within is still good. See the treasure.

How does the Holy Spirit correct us?

Here's a simple test to see if you are getting this: What comes to mind when you hear the word *correction*? Do you think of a mistake that needs to be punished? Do you think of the "rod of correction" and naughty boys in need of a whipping? If you do, God bless you, but your thinking is influenced by the old covenant (see Proverbs 22:15).

In the Old Testament, God's correction was thought to involve the application of the proverbial rod to the seat of learning. It meant punishment and sickness sent in response to sin. At least that's how David understood it:

> Remove your plague from me; I am consumed by the blow of your hand. When with rebukes you correct man for iniquity, you make his beauty melt away like a moth. Surely every man is vapor. (Psalm 39:10–11, NKJV)

Under the law-keeping covenant, the chastisement of the Lord was sometimes fatal. If you sinned, you were toast. Thank God for the new covenant of grace! Under grace your sins are toast, not you. This means we need a new definition of correction.

When I hear the word *correction* I think of a sailboat heading in a dangerous direction. A course correction is needed. The sailboat isn't necessarily sinning or wrong. The sailboat's sin is not the point. You can curse the map and apply the rod of correction to the satnav box but that won't accomplish anything. Far better to just get back on course.

In the new covenant the word for *correction* means "a straightening up again."[3] Isn't that wonderful? It implies all is not lost. You may have missed Jesus and veered off course, but your life is not over. You may be heading towards the rocks or you may have already sunk your boat, but the Holy Spirit can still straighten you up again.

In my earlier example I was a bad dad. From time to time I'm also a bad husband. (Don't judge me. I'm just being honest.) I am not always the shining knight Camilla married. When I say or do something that wounds my wife, how does the Holy Spirit correct me? Here's what he doesn't do: He doesn't accuse me of wrongdoing or condemn me as a sinner, he doesn't dump a bucket of guilt all over me, and he doesn't chastise me with the blows of sickness to teach me a lesson.

Instead, he gently lets me know that I am sowing death into my marriage. Like a lighthouse keeper, he illuminates the dangerous rocks ahead of me. When realization dawns, it is natural for me to feel like a jerk. "I am a terrible husband and chief of sinners." And when that happens the Holy Spirit is right there to remind me that I am still the righteousness of God in Christ Jesus.

If you need an example of Holy Spirit-correction from the Bible, consider the Galatians.

> You were doing so well until someone made you turn from the truth. (Galatians 5:7, CEV)

The Galatians had started well then veered off course. They left the gospel of grace and took a left turn back to the law. They needed to be straightened up again.

How did the Holy Spirit bring about a course correction? Did he send a plague? Did he make them all sick? Of course not! Instead, he inspired Paul to write one of the best books in the Bible, namely, the epistle to the Galatians.

In the old covenant, godly correction was often terrifying. But in the new, it is always beautiful. The Galatians were foolish, but God didn't write them off. Instead, he turned their folly into an opportunity to shine a bright light on Jesus and bless us all by giving us a book that has been called the Magna Carta of Christian liberty.

That's what God does. He turns our messes and mistakes into redemptive launch pads for his grace and glory, leaving us speechless with wonder and adoration.

What happens if we don't respond to the Holy Spirit's correction?

In the walk of life, the Holy Spirit will seek to guide us into all truth and bring about a course correction when we begin to stray. But what happens if we don't heed him? What happens if we persist in a dangerous direction? In this case the Holy Spirit will intensify his warning to the point of bringing a rebuke:

> My son, do not despise the chastening of the Lord, nor be discouraged when you are rebuked by him. (Hebrews 12:5b NKJV)

Understand that the Lord doesn't rebuke you for your sin. He doesn't scream, "Look at what you did!" God is not a faultfinder. But he will warn you when your little sailboat is heading towards trouble. "Look where you are heading. Watch out for those rocks!"

We can see the threefold work of the Holy Spirit—his guiding, correcting, and rebuking—in the Ephesian church. When Paul first went to Ephesus, he met twelve men who identified themselves as followers of John. They were godly men but they hadn't heard about Jesus (see Acts 19:1-7). They weren't walking in all truth. They needed the Holy Spirit's guidance and, through Paul, they got it. The result was a new church.

Sometime later Paul wrote a letter to the Ephesian Christians. Since this letter is nicer than some of the letters he wrote to other churches, it's tempting to picture the Ephesians as model believers. Yet Paul's letter is not without urgings and gentle corrections. For instance, Paul told them he had been praying they would get a deeper revelation of Jesus (Ephesians 1:17-23). And he was also praying that they would know the fathomless love of God that surpasses knowledge (Ephesians 3:14-19). Paul was saying, "You guys are doing so well. Even so, my prayer is that you would know God's love more than you do." What does that tell you? It tells you the Ephesians were in danger of drifting from God's love. And that's exactly what happened.

Fast forward to Revelation 2 and we find the Ephesians have well and truly wandered from the love of God. They have gotten so busy doing religious stuff that they have become loveless and graceless. This is a disaster, a catastrophe. They are now well past the need for guidance and gentle correction. What they need is a full-blown rebuke, and that's exactly what Jesus gives them (Revelation 2:4–6).

Jesus says they have forsaken their first love and need to remember the height from which they have fallen. In other words, they need to turn their ship around and return to the high place of God's love and grace.

In the old covenant, a godly rebuke was always terrifying, as it invariably carried the threat of punishment. But in the new, a rebuke from the Lord is not to be feared. It's a sign that your Father loves you enough to get involved in the details of your life. Jesus doesn't threaten the Ephesians with divine punishment. Instead he warns them of what lies ahead before reminding them of his promises to overcomers.

God's grace cannot be extinguished by your sins and mistakes. The good news declares that if you do make a purple-crayon mess of your life, your heavenly Father still loves you, he still cares for you, and he will never kick you out of his family.

12. Is Grace a License to Sin?

Jesus was a friend of sinners. He ate in their homes and danced at their parties. He did this to show that God loves us all, regardless of who we are. And he did it to demonstrate that God's grace is for sinners. It's not for those who act holier than thou. Grace is for losers. It's for addicts, abusers, drunkards, embezzlers, gamblers, gossips, gluttons, liars, crooks, swindlers, and spammers. Grace is for bad dads and frazzled moms and wayward daughters and prodigal sons. Grace is for those who need it.

Religion, unlike Jesus, is no friend of sinners. Religion says God may love you if you act right, talk right, and hang out with the right sort of people. Religion will tell you that grace isn't for sinners, but winners. It's for those who play by the rules, color inside the lines, and do what they're told. In other words, grace is for those who don't need it.

If you are struggling with sin, you probably know that religion is not your friend. But you may not know that Jesus is the best friend you'll ever have. He's not allergic to your sin and he won't break out in hives when he hears what you've done. Instead, he'll probably say, "Let's have dinner. I'll bring the wine."

Can you imagine what it would've been like for those first-century sinners who had Jesus around for a meal? Can you imagine the questions they would've asked him? Possibly, they would've asked questions like those in this book. What is God like? Can God heal me? How can I be free?

And maybe they would have asked questions like these ...

Will God love me if I keep sinning?

I heard a pastor of a large church tell his congregation, "God hates you, God is sick of you, God is frustrated with you, God is weary of you." And why is God in such a dark mood? Because of our sin and apathy. Jesus went through hell for us, but we can't even show up to church on time.

I wish sermons like this were rare, but they are not. Religious manipulators love to frighten those Christ died for because those who are afraid are easier to control.

The truth is, God loves you like crazy. He loves you when you're up and he loves you when you're down. He loves you when you get it right and he loves you when you get it wrong. Whether you're preaching condemnation from the pulpit or receiving it in the pew, he loves you.

"But Paul, does he love me when I sin?" Aren't you listening? Haven't you seen the cross?

> The proof of God's amazing love is this: that it was while we were sinners that Christ died for us. (Romans 5:8, Phillips)

You need to settle this in your heart. God loves you. Period. Whether you're in the zone or the gutter, the one constant you can count on is your Father's unwavering love for you.

1 Corinthians 13 gives one of the best descriptions of God's love.

> Love endures long and is patient and kind ... it endures everything [without weakening]. Love never fails [never fades out or becomes obsolete or comes to an end]. (1 Corinthians 13:4,7–8, AMP)

The love of men is frail and weak but your Father's love endures forever (Psalm 136). The real question is not whether God will always love you but whether you know and enjoy his love.

Every one of us needs our Father's hugs. Every one of us needs a home where we are loved for who we are. If you have not found a home in your Father's embrace, your legitimate desire for love and acceptance will lead you to inferior sources, like dead religion.

The strange thing about that "God hates you" sermon was that it came packaged as a message of love. "God loves you, but he hates you." Why do people listen to such nonsense? Because they hunger for love. If bearing God's anger and hatred is the price his love, they'll pay it. It's a tragedy. We need love, God has love, but between us is the pimp of religion, prostituting the love of God and charging us for what is already ours in Christ.

Don't listen to his diabolical sales talk. Don't let him tell you that your sins are causing God to withhold his love from you. Listen instead to the gospel of God's grace and acceptance:

> Do you think anyone is going to be able to drive a wedge between us and Christ's love for us? There is no way! Not trouble, not hard times, not hatred, not hunger, not homelessness, not bullying threats, not backstabbing, not even the worst sins listed in scripture. (Romans 8:35, MSG)

Will I lose my salvation if I keep sinning?

"If you keep sinning as a Christian, you're worse off than when you started," says the religious fearmonger. "Forget about repentance. The only thing you can expect is judgment and raging fire. It's all in Hebrews."

I don't want to minimize the warnings of Hebrews, but they are not for Christians. Can you lose your salvation if you keep sinning? Let me put it to you this way: Can you win your salvation if you don't? The answer to one is the answer to the other, and that answer is no.

Just as your righteous acts don't qualify you, your unrighteous acts don't disqualify you. Jesus is your salvation, and the Holy Spirit within is your eternal guarantee (2 Corinthians 1:22).

But this question raises another. What is salvation? Religion defines salvation as something to be experienced in the distant future. Do well now and you may be saved later. The problem with this is it leaves us so obsessed with making heaven and avoiding hell that we put life on hold. We mortgage our lives for an uncertain future.

In contrast, the gospel declares salvation is not there and then; it's here and now. Today is the day of salvation (2 Corinthians 6:2). Life is not about avoiding sin and hell any more than marriage is about avoiding adultery and divorce. Real life is knowing God in the moment (John 17:3). It's walking with him in the shared adventure of life as he defines it. This is the message of the gospel—not that you can experience heaven in the future, but that you can experience heaven on earth today. It's a whole new way of living.

What does this have to do with sin? The cheap thrills of sin cannot hold a candle to the deeper joys of the kingdom. Those who have tasted the goodness of God are no longer satisfied by sin. Sin doesn't attract because they have found something better.

If God loves me, why can't I keep doing what I'm doing?

Because sin is stupid. It's like texting on the freeway or parking on the train track. Just because you can doesn't mean you should.

> For he who sows to his own flesh (lower nature, sensuality) will from the flesh reap decay and ruin and destruction, but he who sows to the Spirit will from the Spirit reap eternal life. (Galatians 6:8, AMP)

There are sheep and there are goats, and there are sheep who act like goats. This scripture isn't preaching works-based salvation. It's saying, "If you're a sheep, don't act like a goat." Walk in the new way of the spirit rather than the old way of the flesh.

If you sow trouble you'll reap trouble. You don't even need to be religious to know this. Everyone knows it's dumb to drink and drive or cheat with another man's wife or lie to the tax man. I have written little about the dangers of sin partly because the dangers are obvious. Sin is its own punishment.

It would be a mistake to conclude that because God loves you he doesn't care about your sin. He cares deeply because sin hurts the object of his affection. God cares about sin because he cares about you.

If God has already forgiven every sin, why can't I keep sinning?

I don't like to discourage questions—I'm all for asking questions—but this is an ignorant question. It's like asking, "Since my gracious wife loves me no matter what, why can't I run after other women?" Why would you want to? You have been given a great feast, so why are you chasing French fries?

A lot of preaching is motivated by the fear of sin. "We have to get sin out of the camp. Gotta make sure it doesn't spread." But we don't have a sin problem. We have an ignorance problem. People sin because they don't appreciate what Christ has done. The remedy is to preach the gospel. The cure for sin is Jesus and his finished work.

It's really very simple: Those who are grateful for the cross don't want to sin. Those who want to sin aren't grateful.

Does God's grace mean I can continue to sin?

Grace brings freedom, and that includes the freedom to make poor choices. But if you use your freedom to enslave yourself again, then what was the point? You have misused grace and are no better off than when you started.

> It is for freedom that Christ has set us free. Stand firm, then, and do not let yourselves be burdened again by a yoke of slavery. (Galatians 5:1)

A Christian who runs after sin is like a prisoner who has been released by a gracious king who then uses his freedom to re-offend and do the things that got him imprisoned in the first place. Now King Jesus is extremely gracious. He won't send you back to prison. But you may send yourself there.

The Galatians used their freedom to enslave themselves to the old law of circumcision. When Paul heard about it, he had a fit. He said, "You've made Christ of no value. You've been alienated from Christ" (see Galatians 5:2, 4).

It's not that Christ had cut them off; they cut themselves off. What kind of Christian cuts themselves off from Christ? Answer: a very dumb Christian.

> Where sin abounded, grace did much more abound. (Romans 5:20b, KJ21)

131

Don't ever fall for the line that says, "I can go on sinning so that grace may abound." True, your sinning won't affect God's love for you, but it will surely affect you. It will enslave and destroy you. This is not God's will for your life. What parent wants to see their kids destroy themselves?

Jesus didn't lead you out of Egypt just so you could run back to Egypt. What would be the point of that? Forget Egypt. There's nothing for you there. You've got better places to go. You've got a land flowing with milk and honey waiting for you, and Jesus wants to take you there.

Is grace is a license to sin?

This is a question people have been asking for as long as the gospel has been preached. It's an ancient question. Here is an ancient answer:

> What shall we say, then? Shall we go on sinning so that grace may increase? By no means! We are those who died to sin; how can we live in it any longer? (Romans 6:1–2)

If you've been liberated by grace, why would you want to run back to that old tyrant of sin? It doesn't make sense.

> So, since we're out from under the old tyranny, does that mean we can live any old way we want? Since we're free in the freedom of God, can we do anything that comes to mind? Hardly. You know well enough from your own experience that there are some acts of so-called freedom that destroy freedom. Offer yourselves to sin, for instance, and it's your last free act. (Romans 6:15–16a, MSG)

Perhaps you've heard stories of people who have taken grace as a license to sin. These stories are sometimes circulated in a misguided attempt to discredit the gospel of grace. While the stories may be awful, they actually have nothing to do with the grace of God which …

... teaches us to say "No" to ungodliness and worldly passions, and to live self-controlled, upright and godly lives in this present age ... (Titus 2:12)

Grace that teaches you to say yes to sin is not the grace of God. It's fake grace. It's like those counterfeit medicines that don't actually do anything.

For the grace of God that brings salvation has appeared to all men. (Titus 2:11, NKJV)

What is the grace of God that has appeared to all men? It's Jesus. Jesus is grace. To say grace promotes licentiousness is to accuse Jesus of teaching us to sin. It's slanderous.

For certain individuals whose condemnation was written about long ago have secretly slipped in among you. They are ungodly people, who pervert the grace of our God into a license for immorality and deny Jesus Christ our only Sovereign and Lord. (Jude 1:4)

Those who interpret grace as a license to sin are anti-Christ and anti-grace. Grace isn't permission to sin; it's the power of God to sin no more.

Why do I still sin?

Sinning follows unbelief. Christians sin either because they are ignorant about their identity in Christ or because they think they have no choice.

The gospel declares you are one with the Lord and in him you are as righteous and holy as he is. But if you don't know you are righteous and holy, you won't act righteous and holy. Consequently, you will do unrighteous and unholy things. Bad behavior follows bad believing.

When it comes to resisting sin, rule-based religion is as useless as a fire hose full of gasoline. It will tell you that if you straighten up and fly right, you can become holy. But that's a faithless flesh-trip. Don't fall for it. Instead, believe the gospel that declares you are a new creation. The old has gone, the new has come, so be holy because that's who you really are.

Maybe you say, "I can't help doing bad things. I couldn't stop even if I wanted to." This is not a wise thing to say. It's a declaration of unbelief in the grace of God that empowers us to say no.

Perhaps you are enslaved to some addiction. You may be in a rut so deep you can't see the sun. But that doesn't mean you are beyond hope and without help. Your Helper is Almighty God. No one is beyond the reach of his transforming grace.

I've met many people who have been healed, delivered, and radically changed by God's grace. When the gospel of grace is preached, this happens all the time. It's normal. But transformation rarely happens among those who don't believe in grace.

If you are bound up with some addiction or habit, stop speaking faithless lies over your life and look instead to your mighty Savior. When you get up in the morning, look at yourself in the mirror and declare, "I am the righteousness of God in Christ Jesus. I am his dearly-loved child." Don't give expression to what the world or religion says about you. Instead, agree with your Father.

And when you're faced with temptation, say it again. When you're about to click on a link you shouldn't click or when you're reaching for something you shouldn't touch, remind yourself: "I am the righteousness of God in Christ Jesus. I am his dearly loved child." This is not the power of positive thinking. This is a frail human being declaring his faith in God's mighty grace.

A couple of months ago a man wrote to tell me how he had been struggling with "multiple sins." At the time he actually despised grace and relied on the guilt of his sins to keep himself in line. When he messed up he would listen to a hyper-holiness preacher so he "could feel miserable and come back to God." But it didn't work. He found himself caught up in an endless cycle of sinning, repenting, and sinning again. One day, in desperation, he cried out to God, and the following scripture came to mind:

For sin shall not have dominion over you, for you are not under law but under grace. (Romans 6:14, NKJV)

From that moment the man quit trying to avoid sin and began trusting in God's grace. He started listening to messages on the unconditional love of the Father and now lives free from the destructive habits of his old lifestyle.

If you are *trying* to do the right thing and *trying* to keep the rules and *trying* to avoid sin, then you can expect to have problems. You're living under self-imposed law. You're trusting in your own puny strength. But if you are *resting* in the grace of God then you can expect to have a breakthrough. It is your God-given, Christ-bought right.

Since I started writing at Escape to Reality, I have heard from many people who have been set free from sin by the grace of God. One man wrote to tell me how he had been delivered from a pornography addiction. He said God opened his eyes to grace using Romans 6 and 7 and "I haven't fallen into the stuff since."

Another man told me how his son heard the gospel of grace and was delivered from heroin addiction and hospital-grade depression. The son now spends his days telling others about the grace of God that saved him.

Stories like these are common in the land of grace for God's grace truly is greater than sin. In contrast, religion is useless in your battle against sin. It fails because it puts the focus on you and relies on the flesh. Like medieval blood-letting, religion sucks you dry making you even more vulnerable to sin. But grace works because it releases the power of God into your situation.

The gospel of grace declares sin *shall not* have dominion over you. It may be that sin presently does have dominion over you, but by the grace of God that reality will soon give way to the superior reality of the kingdom. So reckon yourself dead to sin, acknowledge every good thing that is yours in Christ Jesus, and get ready to receive your breakthrough. Let grace be your license to sing.

13. Is It God's Will for Me to Be Sick?

When Camilla and I started pastoring in the late 1990s, we didn't have a clue. We loved God with all our hearts and we prayed a lot, but our prayers seldom moved mountains. On one occasion there was a lot of sickness going around so we organized a healing meeting. We laid hands on the sick, prayed like mad, but nobody got healed. In fact, after the meeting more people got sick!

We joke about it now, but we weren't laughing then. Why was it so hard to heal people? I have since come to understand that many sincere believers struggle to receive healing because of false teaching. They've been told it's not God's will to heal everyone or that God uses sickness to teach character or that God used to heal people, but now he's retired. Others struggle because they simply don't know how to pray for the sick. Nobody's taught them. We didn't know, but we learned. You can too.

Is it always God's will to heal?

When Joseph learned that his fiancée, Mary, was pregnant, he decided to call off the wedding. But an angel came to him with a message that would change everything for everyone forever:

> Joseph son of David, do not be afraid to take Mary home as your wife, because what is conceived in her is from the Holy Spirit. She will give birth to a son, and you are to give him the name Jesus, because he will save his people from their sins. (Matthew 1:20b–21)

Here are three things from heaven: a messenger with a name, a baby, and a mission. The heavenly messenger told Joseph that Mary's son was not conceived by natural means but by the Holy Spirit. "This is one special kid, Joe. Like no other ever born." He said the son was to be called Jesus. "You know what that means, right Joe? It means 'the Lord who saves.'" And then he said that the son would save people. "Are you following me Joseph? Mary's son from heaven is 'the Lord who saves' who saves."

It's like God was trying to tell us something.

137

But what does it mean to save? The word *save* first uttered by the angel is the Greek word *sozo*, which means to deliver or protect, heal or preserve. It means to make whole.[1]

Jesus, the Savior from heaven, came to make broken people whole. How could this not include healing and deliverance? Forgiveness from sin is wonderful, but it's only part of the package. Jesus wants to do a complete number on you. He wants to deliver you from sin and all its cursed effects.

> Praise the Lord, my soul, and forget not all his benefits — who forgives all your sins and heals all your diseases. (Psalm 103:2-3)

If you don't know Jesus heals, you are missing out on some of his benefits. You're not getting the full bang for his buck. You're not enjoying everything he's given you. Your grasp of *sozo* is so-so. You need to enlarge your understanding of God and how mighty he is. If he is mighty to save he is mighty to heal, for the two are interchangeable. They are both expressions of *sozo*.

In the Bible you will find stories of people receiving salvation in the form of healing from "the Lord who saves." Here's one:

> Then one of the synagogue rulers, named Jairus, came there. Seeing Jesus, he fell at his feet and pleaded earnestly with him, "My little daughter is dying. Please come and put your hands on her so that she will be healed (*sozo*) and live." (Mark 5:22-23)

Jesus set off to heal the sick girl but on the way was detained by a woman who had been bleeding for twelve years.

> When she heard about Jesus, she came up behind him in the crowd and touched his cloak, because she thought, "If I just touch his clothes, I will be healed (*sozo*)." (Mark 5:27-28)

And she was. The woman reached out to Jesus and was healed of a long-term affliction. She was *sozo*-ed. But then bad news. A messenger arrived to tell Jairus his little girl had died.

Hearing this, Jesus said to Jairus, "Don't be afraid; just believe, and she will be healed (*sozo*)." (Luke 8:50)

And he did and she was.

We tend to compartmentalize forgiveness and healing, but Jesus just sees salvation. A paraplegic is brought to him, and Jesus says, "Cheer up, your sins are forgiven." And then for good measure, he heals him (see Matthew 9:1–7). Do you see? Jesus dealt with his sins *and* his sickness. That's *sozo*. That's making a broken person whole.

God's will for salvation is God's will for healing. There is no difference. Since God wants all to be saved we can be assured that God wants all to be healed. Jesus is proof of this. Every sick person who came to Jesus was healed (e.g., Matthew 12:15).

Jesus never doubted that God's will is always to heal, and neither should you. Don't ever pray, "Lord heal me, *if it be thy will*." This is not a prayer of faith, but doubt and uncertainty. Instead, pray according to his will, which is to heal every single person every single time.

Jesus taught us to pray to God like this: "Let your will be done on earth as it is in heaven." There is no sickness in heaven because God is on the throne and where he reigns, sickness cannot endure. His will for there is his will for here.

Where does sickness come from?

When God made the world it was good. There was no sin, no death, and no sickness. All that bad stuff came because man listened to a lie and opened a door to trouble.

> Sin entered the world through one man, and death through sin, and in this way death came to all people, because all sinned. (Romans 5:12)

Sickness is death in installments. If your pancreas malfunctions or your memory fades, we may call it diabetes or Alzheimer's, but it's actually a foretaste of death. It's a part of you that is no longer working as God intended.

We have lived with sickness and death for so long that it has become normal, but Jesus did not accept sickness as normal. He rebuked it with authority. Nor did Jesus wonder whether sickness was the result of bad genes or stress or an unhealthy diet. He knew that all sickness ultimately originates with that old thief the devil.

> The thief comes only to steal and kill and destroy; I have come that they may have life, and have it to the full. (John 10:10)

Have you been robbed of your health? Have you suffered loss? Don't blame God. It's the thief who has robbed you. I have heard people with long-term illnesses say, "I have made peace with my condition." Forgive me, but that's like making peace with the devil. The hemorrhaging woman suffered for many years, but she never accepted her condition as normal. If she had she would not have reached out to Jesus with faith.

If you are suffering, don't sit there and take it like a passive, pitiful Job. Instead, follow Jesus, who resisted the enemy by healing the sick.

> You know of Jesus of Nazareth, how God anointed him with the Holy Spirit and with power, and how he went about doing good and healing all who were oppressed by the devil, for God was with him. (Acts 10:38, NASB)

Like vomit on a classic painting, sickness is an affront to the goodness of a good Creator. It's a Satanic stain on us, his living masterpieces. We were created in God's image. We were glorious. And then the devil showed up with his spray can of sin and sickness. The devil is the biggest vandal there is, but the good news is Jesus came to destroy his work.

> He drove out the spirits with a word and healed all the sick. (Matthew 8:16b)

Jesus healed the sick, he commanded his disciples to heal the sick (Matthew 10:8), and he said we would heal the sick (Mark 16:18).

So why are we unsure about his will for the sick? His will is that we heal them.

Does God make us sick to teach us things?

A few months ago I fell off a ladder and broke a rib. It was an incredible learning experience. I learned one should not climb a ladder that is resting on a flimsy branch. And I learned how every little thing hurts when your ribs are busted.

Experience is an effective but brutal teacher. So is sickness. But God doesn't need either to teach you. Jesus said the Holy Spirit would teach us "all things" (John 14:26). If we can learn all things through the Holy Spirit, what is left for us to learn from sickness?

God is certainly able to take life's hardships and make them work out for good, but he doesn't give us the hardships in the first place. God didn't push me off that ladder and he'll never give you cancer to teach you humility.

Under the old covenant, people got sick as a consequence of breaking the law. Under the law, sickness and disease were clearly identified as curses (see Deuteronomy 28:15–28). But Jesus has redeemed us from the curse of the law that we might live healthy and abundant lives.

Don't ever think God is making you sick to punish you or that he's "allowing" a sickness to teach you stuff. Instead, have the mind of Christ. Jesus had a zero-tolerance policy when it came to sickness. Jesus took sickness *off* people; he didn't give it to them.

How do we heal the sick?

Much of what passes for prayer is wishful thinking. "Oh Lord, please heal Mary." *I'm sure you can, Lord. I just don't know if you will.* "I beg you to heal Tom." *But if you do, no one will be more surprised than me.* You can pretty much guarantee these sorts of prayers won't change anything because they are devoid of faith.

> The prayer offered in faith will make the sick person well; the Lord will raise them up. (James 5:15a)

If you are not sure that God will answer your prayers, he probably won't (see James 1:6–7). You may hope that he does, but faith is not hope. Faith is being sure of what we hope for and certain of what we don't yet see (Hebrews 11:1).

Jairus came to Jesus certain that he could heal his daughter. The woman who had been bleeding was just as certain that Jesus could make her whole. You need to be certain too.

There are no formulas or magic prayers for healing the sick. There is only faith in God. Our faith doesn't manufacture the healing or compel God to heal us. Rather, faith is the means by which we access the abundant provision of his grace. Faith is simply agreeing with God. That's how we receive. If you don't agree you'll have a much harder time receiving.

Two blind men came to Jesus looking for healing (see Matthew 9:27–30). Jesus asked them, "Do you believe I can do this?" "Yes, Lord," they replied. Jesus then touched their eyes and said, "According to your faith it will be done to you," and their sight was restored.

Look carefully at the faith of these two blind men. How many days had they fasted and prayed? None. For how long had they pounded the gates of heaven with persistent prayers? They hadn't. Yet they had enough faith to get the job done. How do we know they had faith? It was evident in the way they spoke. They came to Jesus with a "Yes, Lord" attitude. They didn't say, "I hope you heal us, Lord," or "If it be your will, Lord." They simply said, "Yes, Lord." That's faith. Faith is agreeing with God. Faith is saying yes to the Lord who saves.

And he himself bore our sins in his body on the cross, so that we might die to sin and live to righteousness; for by his wounds you were healed. (1 Peter 2:24, NASB)

This verse looks like a misprint. *Were healed? I'm not healed, Peter. I'm sick as a dog.* But as far as the work of healing you goes, everything that needed to be done has been done.

Jesus bore your sins, *past tense*. Jesus bore your sicknesses, *past tense*. You have been forgiven, *past tense*. You have been healed, *past tense*. Your present reality may not reflect it, but the grace you need for your healing has already been given. How are we to respond? With faith! Faith is being certain of what you don't yet see. Faith is giving thanks for what Christ has done. Faith is the means through which his grace will transform your present reality into his saving reality.

How do we pray with faith?

> So then faith comes by hearing, and hearing by the word of God. (Romans 10:17, NKJV)

The word of God is Jesus. Faith comes when we hear about Jesus. That hemorrhaging woman suffered for twelve years before faith came. What happened in the twelfth year? "She heard about Jesus" (Mark 5:27). Someone told her about the Lord who saves and she believed what she heard.

Perhaps as you are reading this chapter, you can feel faith stirring within you. This is a normal reaction to hearing about Jesus. If you are sick, or if there's a part of your body that has succumbed to death and disease, and you have faith in Jesus, lay hands on yourself right now. Take this opportunity to receive from the riches of his grace. Pray for yourself with faith and boldness. You don't need to talk to God about your sickness — he already knows. Instead, talk to your sickness about your God. Speak to your mountain. Faith doesn't move God; faith moves mountains. Command that sickness to go!

Since faith comes by hearing about Jesus, when I pray I like to remind myself of who Jesus is and what he has done. I might say, "Thank you Lord that your name is above every other name. You are greater than this sickness. You have already provided everything I need to be healed, so I'll just receive it."

There's no right or wrong way to do this, but a prayer of faith will be characterized by thanksgiving and praise. It takes no faith to complain about your woes. It takes faith to thank God in advance for his healing and grace.

If you struggle to get your focus off yourself, consider the cross where Christ bore our infirmities and sorrows. Then consider the empty tomb that testifies to the supernatural power of a God who raises the dead.

Got any healing stories?

Once you've seen Jesus, believing is easy. The hard part is resting in that place of trust while you wait for the healing to manifest.

I once received a phone call from a tradesman who was doing some renovations on my house. He hadn't shown up for work and was calling to let me know where he was. In a broken voice he told me he was in the hospital sitting outside the intensive care unit. "My brother's been in a motorcycle accident. He hit his head, and the doctors say he's not going to make it." The despair in his voice was palpable. It was clear that he had given up his brother for dead.

As I heard the diagnosis of death, something inside me stirred. It was faith in the form of a holy indignation. Bold words came to my mouth. "Listen, you don't know this, but I'm a Christian. That means when I pray for the sick, they get healed. Can I pray for your brother now, over the phone?" He agreed, and in the name of Jesus, I commanded life over his comatose brother and the complete restoration of all his mental faculties. I kept it short, he thanked me for praying, and then I heard nothing for 72 hours.

The morning after I prayed the following thought came to my mind. *Boy, you sure were bold yesterday. You are going to look silly when this man dies. And he will die. You heard what the doctors said.* My shoulders slumped, and for about two seconds I felt depressed. That's how long it took to discern the death-dealing spirit behind the thought. "Wait a second," I said to myself. "This thought is not of God. It is not the Lord's will for this man to die." I chose not to agree with that dark thought but took it captive and made it bow to King Jesus. Then I shouted at nobody in particular, "This man will not die but live!" Two days later he was discharged from the ICU and on his way to a full recovery.

Everything we need for healing was made available through the sacrifice of God's Son. So why aren't more people healed? One reason is they are living under law.

Paul said the law is a ministry of death (2 Corinthians 3:7). Live by the law and it will make you sick and then it will kill you. If you think you are sick because you are being judged for some sin, or if you think you have to fast and pray and otherwise earn your healing, then you are living under law. Your beliefs are literally making you sick and keeping you from receiving the healing that comes by grace alone.

Live under the law and you may experience crippling stress, anxiety, even full-blown depression. I personally know many people who have suffered terrible illnesses as a direct result of trying to be good Christians. The problem is not Christ or Christianity—it's DIY religion. It's the mindset that says you have to work to make yourself into a new person. The problem is you can't succeed and you may die trying. The endless cycle of dedication, failure, and recommitment can literally break your mind and body.

The law makes you sick, but the good news is that grace can make you better![2]

This week I heard from a lady who battles with a type of OCD known as scrupulosity. This is a mental disorder characterized by guilt over religious issues. This lady had been to "countless therapists," but nothing had helped. Then she read something I wrote about God's great grace and felt her fears calm for the first time in a long time. I can promise you it was not my eloquent writing that set her free! It was the good news of grace revealed in Jesus.

Jesus said, "According to your faith it will be done to you." I know people who are convinced God does not heal, and guess what, they never see anyone get healed. I know others who believe he does, and they do. Who would you rather be? The unbelieving cynic who buries their loved ones with the satisfaction of knowing they were right? Or the believer who may not see miracles every time but surely sees them some of the time? I'd rather be a part-time healer than a full-time doubter. I'd rather walk with those who are seeing the kingdom come than sit on the sidelines with those who only read about it.

What is Jesus' medicine?

My five-year-old daughter came home from school with a fever. We wrapped her up in her quilt, made her comfortable on the couch, and prayed for her. She got worse. By the time dinner was served, she was lying on the floor moaning and unable to get up.

It was time for Jesus' medicine!

It might surprise you to learn that in the cupboard we have some divine medicine that is super effective for healing. It goes by the name of communion, which for my daughter meant black-currant cordial and pita bread. There is nothing special about pita bread, but there is something very special about proclaiming the Lord's death — which is what we are doing whenever we take communion.

When we proclaim the Lord's death, we are saying Christ died to deliver us from sin and all the effects of sin, including sickness. We are agreeing with the prophet who said:

Surely he took up our pain and bore our suffering ... and by his wounds we are healed. (Isaiah 53:4–5)

In chapter 10, we looked at the benefits of communion and how Paul's instructions to the Corinthians are sometimes used to withhold grace from those who need it most. One reason why some people hesitate to partake of communion is because of what Paul says here:

For those who eat and drink without discerning the body of Christ eat and drink judgment on themselves. That is why many among you are weak and sick, and a number of you have fallen asleep. (1 Corinthians 11:29–30)

In context, Paul is speaking about the negative judgment unbelievers bring on themselves by refusing grace. But then he makes a point that's relevant to Christians. He basically says, "We may suffer too, not because God condemns us, but because we condemn ourselves through unbelief."

An "unbelieving believer" ought to be a contradiction in terms, but it's not. An unbelieving believer is the Christian who thinks he must keep the rules to stay healthy. It's the mother worried sick about her children. It's the miserable minister busting his hump for the Lord.

An unbelieving believer is any Christian who relies on their own resources and understanding instead of relying on the Lord. It's an unhealthy way to live.

> But if we judged ourselves rightly, we would not be judged. But when we are judged, we are disciplined by the Lord so that we will not be condemned along with the world. (1 Corinthians 11:31–32, NASB)

The word for *disciplined* in this verse should not make you think of punishment. It means training as in training up a child. Paul is saying, "When we renew our minds and learn to discern what is from the Lord and what is not, we are trained up as sons and daughters and no longer suffer the effects of sin and condemnation."[3]

When we get ill we need to ask ourselves, "Is this sickness from the Lord?" When we come under pressure and stress, same thing. "Is this anxiety I am experiencing from the Lord?" Then, once we have renewed our minds — *this bad thing is not from God* — we are ready to proclaim the Lord's death over our situation. "Christ died that I might enjoy a healthy life. Sickness, leave! Anxiety, take a hike!"

Taking communion when you're sick is great way to exercise your God-given faith. It's saying, "I don't identify with these symptoms. I identify with Jesus, who carried my infirmities and was wounded that I might be healed."

When my kids get sick, it makes me sick. My natural flesh responds with fear and anxiety and I cannot rest. But one place I find comfort is in these two words from Isaiah: "Surely, he ..." Surely he took up our infirmities. Surely he carried our sorrows and sicknesses.

My feverish daughter was lying sick and moaning on the floor. As a family we took communion together and proclaimed the

Lord's death over her. We thanked Jesus for carrying her infirmities and then commanded the sickness to go. The change was dramatic. Within a minute she perked up. The fever left and she went to the table and wolfed down her meal. Then she had seconds. She was her usual cheerful self and when she went to bed later that evening she thanked Jesus for healing her.

Hand on heart, I have to admit we don't see such miraculous healings every time we pray. But one thing we have learned is that we are more likely to see healings when we pray than when don't. We may be part-time healers, but our desire is to reveal Jesus the full-time healer every time we pray.

The bad news of life says sickness and death are inevitable. The worse news of religion says you can hasten your own demise by trusting in the death-dealing law and engaging in dead works. But the good news of grace says death no longer has the last word. Jesus is the Author of new life. In him we have a Healer who is greater than any hurt and a Savior mightier than death.

14. Is God's Love Conditional on My Obedience?

If God loves us unconditionally, how do we account for those scriptures that link his love with our obedience, like this one?

> If you love me, you will keep my commandments. (John 14:15, NASB)

A legalist reads this backwards: "You will keep my commandments, *if* you love me." In other words, you must prove your love for Christ by obeying him. But one who is walking in grace reads it as Jesus said it. He understands that obedience is a byproduct of knowing Christ's love.

This is no small distinction. In fact, it is the difference between life and death.

If you are confused about your Father's love, you will tie yourself up in knots over this issue of obedience. You'll be susceptible to the lie that says your relationship with God is defined by what you do. I'm talking about the mindset that says, "You can't love Jesus without embracing a lifestyle of obedience. If you're not obeying, you're not loving. If you want to be known as one who loves Jesus, you'd better do what he says."

This is twisted. It's completely back to front. Our relationship with Jesus is love-based not task-based. Genuine obedience follows love. Obedience is a fruit, not a root.

What is the root of obedience?

The other day I was walking with my girls to a playground. We were walking along a waterfront esplanade that is sometimes used by goods vehicles. My girls were ahead of me and with all the noise and excitement, they didn't notice a van approaching from the right. In a loud voice I told them to stop and they did.

Like good Kiwi kids, they then instinctively looked to their left for the vehicle they knew must be coming, only they could see no car. It would've been funny if it hadn't been dangerous. They were both straining so hard to look left that they were oblivious to the van approaching on their right.

Forgive the dramatization, but at this point each of my girls faced a life-threatening choice: to walk by sight (*I see no car*) or by faith (*but Daddy told me to stop*). They were itching to get on to the playground, but their trust in me kept them safe and still. Well to be honest, the younger one needed encouraging, but you get my point. They obeyed me because they trust me. See the connection? Genuine obedience follows trust, which is based on love.

Anyone who loves me will obey my teaching. (John 14:23a)

If A, then B. If you love someone you will trust them and heed what they say. That's what Jesus is saying here. It's obvious, isn't it? Here's the flipside:

Anyone who does not love me will not obey my teaching. (John 14:24a)

If you don't love someone, you won't heed what they say. Again, this is obvious, right?

Only it's *not* obvious, for many are trying to obey God out of fear instead of love. Why fear? Because they've been told they have to obey and avoid sin and do everything the Bible says because if they don't, God will reject them. They will be cast aside with the weeds, told to depart with the goats, and burned with the unfruitful branches. It's terrifying stuff.

It's always a good idea to avoid sin, but if you think Jesus died to turn you into a do-gooder and that he uses terror to compel your compliance, you have missed the mark by a million miles. There is no fear in love. My girls didn't stop on the side of the road because they are afraid of me. Neither should you be afraid of your loving Father.

If you keep my commands, you will remain in my love, just as I have kept my Father's commands and remain in his love. (John 15:10)

Again, this looks like Jesus is preaching conditional love. Only he isn't. Read the preceding verse:

As the Father has loved me, so have I loved you. Now remain in my love. (John 15:9)

How does the Father love the Son? Unconditionally. Before Jesus had done a blessed thing, God said, "This is my beloved Son" (Matthew 3:17). "Do you see how my Father loves me?" says Jesus. "That's how I love you." Jesus is proclaiming his unconditional love for us. This is good news. This should make you smile.

Christ's love is a rock-solid foundation you can build on. But you won't have a rock-solid life unless you receive it. Hence the exhortation that follows:

Remain in my love. Abide, dwell, stay permanently in my love. Sink your roots deep and let nothing move you from my love. Don't let the insecure try and sell you my love. Look to the cross — you already have my love. Other loves will disappoint but my love never fails. My love is the one constant that will hold your world together if you receive it, so receive it. Bask in it, bathe in it, swim in it, stay in it. (John 15:9, Paul's paraphrase)

That's the best, most blessed news in the universe. It's the news a loveless world most needs to hear. Perhaps you've heard it before, but you need to preach this good news to yourself every single day. *Jesus loves me. He really loves me.*

Then, when you are secure in the foundation of verse 9, you can go on and read verse 10, which I paraphrase like this: "Trusting me to the point of doing what I say is a sign you are remaining in my love."

The issue isn't obedience versus disobedience. It's trust versus distrust. When you know how much your Father loves you, you will trust and obey him naturally.

What happens if we don't remain in his love?

Return with me to the esplanade. Do you see my girls standing obediently, still and safe? Here is the $64,000 question: What holds them still when they want to run on? There is only one thing — my love for them.

Because my girls know how much I love them, they trust me to make decisions for them. I can see things they can't see, like oncoming vans. It's the same with your heavenly Father. He loves you so much that you can trust him with your life.

But what if one of my girls is having a bad day? Perhaps she got out of bed on the wrong side. Perhaps she is hungry and irritable. What if she is no longer remaining in my love? She might start thinking, *Why do I have to stop? I don't need anyone to tell me what to do. I'm not stopping. I'm going to run on to the playground.*

So she runs out in front of the van. This is not good! Her disobedience could get her killed. But I would not be the one killing her.

Again, this is obvious, right? So why do we think God punishes us when we disobey him? The heavy van of life knocks us down, and as we lay bleeding we tell ourselves, "God is chastising me." Only he's not. He didn't give you cancer, make you redundant, or cause your spouse to run off with the kids. God is almighty, but that doesn't make him responsible for everything that happens to you.

You need to understand that your Father loves you when you're obedient and he loves you when you're disobedient. His love never changes. But we change. We may wander from the sunshine of his love to the shade of self-trust. When that happens, we put ourselves in danger. We make stupid decisions, listen to lies, and reap the whirlwind.

If my daughter disobeys me she might get flattened by the van, but I won't kick her out of the family. Neither will God kick you out of his family when you disobey. His eternal love is greater than your momentary lapses of judgment.

"Paul, are you saying that my obedience doesn't matter?"

Of course it matters. Obeying God will keep you from getting splattered by the proverbial truck. Jesus councils us to remain in his love because that's our home. His love is your strong tower and refuge.

We don't obey to earn his love (we already have it) or his forgiveness (in Christ, it's already ours). We obey our heavenly

Father for the same reason my girls obeyed me the other evening: Because we know he is good and he loves us and wants the best for us.

Why did Adam fall?

> Adam disobeyed God and suffered the consequences. Jesus has given us a second chance—don't screw it up this time. God demands total obedience. The devil will do what he can to make you disobey because he knows that "God's wrath comes on those who are disobedient." So do what you're told and obey.

Right there is your standard sermon on obedience. Have you heard it before? Okay, maybe my version is a little heavy-handed and over the top. Maybe the version you heard was more tactful and came with mood music and an altar call. But if the punchline was, "You must obey God *or else,*" then what you heard was pure law.

I hope you understand that by "law," I don't necessarily mean the Ten Commandments. Law is anything *you must do* to make God love you or bless you or accept you. "We must embrace a lifestyle of obedience if we are to please the Lord." That's law. "If you would follow Jesus you must obey his word." This too is law.

Any law-based message will leave you wondering, "How does the love of God figure into this?" The law-preacher has a ready answer. "Jesus said if you love me you will obey me. To love God means to obey his commands. God is to be feared and obeyed." That sounds scary. That sounds like the love of God hinges on my perfect obedience and, to be honest, I am not perfectly obedient. If I disobey, does that mean God won't accept me? Does that mean I'm not truly saved?

Bingo.

Now the law-preacher has you right where he wants you—sitting on the edge of your seat, anxious and ready to swallow whatever list of dead works he has for you today. Using fiery rhetoric and chopped-up scriptures, he will whip you into a frenzy of promise making. "Lord, I'll do everything the Bible says."

Do you know what happens next? Well, if your flesh is strong, you'll be singled out as a walking-talking Christian success story, and your ego will get a hefty injection of religious pride. But if your flesh is weak, you'll be marginalized as a failure and shackled with guilt and condemnation. Either way you lose.

"Paul, are you against obedience?" I am not. I am against flesh-powered Christianity. I am against anything that smells of self-trust.

To get to the heart of this obedience issue we need to go back to the beginning, to the Garden of Eden. To get the right answer, we need to ask the right question, which is this: Why did Adam fall? For many years, my answer to that question was: "Adam disobeyed God." That seems simple enough, doesn't it? God told Adam not to eat; Adam ate. End of story.

Only it's not the end of the story. It's not even the right story. Adam's disobedience was not the problem but a symptom of a deeper problem, which is that he did not trust God. In eating the forbidden fruit, Adam declared God to be an untrustworthy liar. Through his actions he was saying, "God, I know better than you. I can decide these matters for myself. I'm better off without you." And so Adam, full of godless wisdom, stepped off the sidewalk right in front of the van called death. Big mistake.

Like us, Adam lived in a world of uncertainty. Like us, he had questions he couldn't answer—questions like these: "Why did God forbid me to eat from this particular tree?" and "What is this 'death' he said would come if I did?"

Adam was in the dark, and that was the whole point. God purposely designed things that way because he wanted Adam and Eve to trust him. By introducing uncertainty into their world, he was inviting them to a relationship of dependence on him. If they had trusted him they would have lived and enjoyed abundant life. But they chose to go their own way and so reaped the awful consequences of their choice.

Life is a setup, an invitation to respond to the overtures of a Creator who loves us and desires to share his life with us. As for Adam, so for us. Think about it. There is far more to life than you can comprehend or manage. You simply don't know how things are going to turn out. You don't know whether your decisions today will prove to be good tomorrow. Have you chosen the right course? Will you still have your job in a year? What will happen if the economy tanks or your health deteriorates? You don't know.

Try as we might we simply weren't made to cope with all that life throws at us. We are designed for dependence. We are hard-wired to trust in a faithful Father who loves us.

Life is big and we are small. But the good news declares that God is biggest of all and he cares for us right down to our smallest needs.

What are the two faces of unbelief?

Obedience follows trust as surely as disobedience follows distrust. But what does distrust look like? Distrust has two aspects: (1) Distrust is Adam disregarding God and saying, "I know better" and (2) distrust is the Israelites at Sinai saying, "God, tell us what to do and we'll do it" (see Exodus 19:8).

Don't be fooled by the Israelites' desire to obey God. Their motives were rotten, and their hearts were faithless. If they trusted God they would not have asked for rules. They would've said, "God, remember your covenant with our father Abraham and bless us." Instead they basically said, "God, we don't believe your promises to Abraham. Tell us how we can bless ourselves." And God gave them what they asked for: rules for self-blessification.

Today there are many who are searching for keys and principles and guidelines and strategies — anything but God himself. They go to church or read their Bibles with an Israelite attitude: "Just tell me what to do and I'll do it."

By idolizing the rules in the Bible or the red letters of Jesus they reveal a faith that is in themselves rather than their Father. This self-trust is evident in a mindset that says, "I will be safe *if I keep the rules*, God will bless me *if I keep the rules*, and God will be pleased with me *if I keep the rules*."

It's as if Jesus never came. It's as if we were still under the old law-keeping covenant. Those who live like this are as faithless as the Israelites. They are rejecting God just as Adam did. Don't you see? Life isn't about rules; it's about relationship.

How does love translate into obedience?

Imagine it's your wedding day. You've had the ceremony, and you're starting to relax when the minister hands you a gift, a thick book of *Marriage Rules*. "Read this," he says. "The secret to a happy marriage is found within." You open the book with interest. Inside you discover many rules and guidelines: "Be honest, be kind, always tell the truth, listen well, keep your promises, say 'please' and 'thank you,' freely forgive, don't covet your neighbor's wife," and that sort of thing. Initially you think, *This is gold! I want a successful marriage, so I will do everything this book says.*

You keep reading and find there are more rules for marriage than you could possibly have imagined. There are rules for special days and different seasons, rules on what to eat and what to wear, rules on property rights, rules regarding intimacy, rules on family planning, and hundreds more. *Phew! I never knew marriage was such hard work. But I want a blessed marriage, so I'll follow the rules. I'll even take this book on our honeymoon.*

But then you turn to the last page and find a surprising message written in large letters:

If you love your spouse, disregard this book. You don't need it.
If you love your spouse, you will keep all the rules effortlessly.

This should be good news. *What relief! I can leave the book at home and enjoy my spouse.* Yet there are some who won't do it. They'll keep the book just in case. But there is no *just in case*. There is no conceivable situation where the rules could replace true love. Do you see? If you love your spouse, you don't need the book, and if you don't love your spouse, all the rules in the world aren't going to help.

Some treat the Bible as though it were a book of rules for how to be married to Jesus. They think they will have a happy marriage if they do everything the Bible says, or at least everything Jesus says. But love doesn't work that way. If you love Jesus, you don't need the rules, and if you don't love Jesus, the rules aren't going to help. Love comes from the heart, not a book. And yet, God help us, we crave rules and instructions. *God, there must be something I can do.* So God in his mercy and patience gives us the mother of all commands:

My command is this: Love each other as I have loved you. (John 15:12)

You want a command to keep? *That's* your command. Do you have a need to do something for Jesus? Then do what he says here: "Love each other." But wait a second. Read the rest of the command: "Love each other *as I have loved you.*"

Right there is grace. Jesus is not giving us law that must be obeyed. Nor is he holding a big stick over our heads and saying, "Love each other to prove you love me." He's saying our love for others can only ever be a response to his love for us. He leads, we follow. He gives, we receive, and only then can we give what we have received.

Do you see the wisdom of Jesus here? If you're the sort of person who craves rules, you will find this one impossible to keep. If you have not experienced his unconditional love, you will struggle to love others. It will be sheer drudgery and you will fail again and again. Read Jesus' words as law, and your need for grace will soon be obvious. "God help me. I can't do it."

Bingo.

Now the Giver of grace has you right where he wants you — at the end of yourself and ready to drink from the fountain of his love. You begin to focus on the second part of his command: *as I have loved you.* You remember the cross and the empty tomb and think of all Jesus has done for you. He has loved you, forgiven you, and wooed you to himself. All this he did before you had done a blessed thing.

Suddenly the penny drops. Grace leaps out of his words and falls on you in a bearlike hug. In an instant, everything changes and you become a different person. A hugged person. A dearly beloved child of God.

As you receive the love of you Father you find you cannot hold it all in. You have to share it with others or you'll burst. "Christ's love compels us," said Paul (2 Corinthians 5:14). It energizes and motivates us. When you have been seized by the power of a great affection it empowers you to love extravagantly. You find that keeping the command of Jesus is easier than breaking it. This is not because grace helps us keep the rules — we may not even know what the rules are — but because Christ lives in us and what Christ says, he does.

15. What Is the Unforgivable Sin?

The nineteenth-century Danish philosopher Søren Kierkegaard was a man cursed by God. Or so he thought, for his father, Michael, had committed the unforgivable sin.

As a child, Michael Kierkegaard was a dirt-poor kid who battled with melancholy. In a moment of weakness, he cursed God for his hardships, thus committing what he believed was an unpardonable sin. He then became a successful businessman, retired young, and lived a long and full life. But the damage had been done. Words had been said. Michael raised his children in the knowledge that God would take revenge. Of course, it never happened. In fact, the Kierkegaards of Copenhagen were healthy and prosperous. But the father's fears shaped the son.

Raised on a diet of strict religion, Søren battled with guilt and wrote despair-ridden books with titles like *The Sickness unto Death*. His angst made him one of the great existential philosophers, but he was not a happy man. Indeed, Kierkegaard was arguably the gloomiest Dane since Hamlet.

I often hear from people who, like Kierkegaard, are worried about the unforgivable sin. They fear they have done something that puts them beyond redemption and hope. Certainly, one of the greatest sources of anxiety is confusion over sin and forgiveness. "Will God forgive me? Have I gone too far?" To the anxious mind the thought that all may be eternally lost is extremely unsettling.

Is there an unforgivable sin? And if so, what is it? Take this question to any Bible commentary and you'll end up with a list of candidate sins such as the one below. The bad news is theologians say one or all of these sins is unpardonable. The good news is theologians are sometimes wrong. You may have committed one or all of the sins on this list, but rest assured that none of them is unforgivable:

1. Having an attitude that calls evil good and good evil
2. Having a lack of reverence
3. Being stubborn and unteachable
4. Not loving the Lord with all your heart, soul, and mind
5. Willfully or habitually sinning

159

6. Having unconfessed sin
7. Having unrepented sin
8. Harboring unforgiveness in your heart
9. Taking the Lord's name in vain
10. Having disrespectful thoughts about the Holy Spirit

There is some bad stuff on this list that can hurt you. For instance, if you harbor unforgiveness, you may end up bitter and twisted. But it is not helpful to tell a young mother whose husband has run off with her best friend that she must forgive him or face eternal damnation. You might as well ask her to walk on water. The power to forgive the unforgivable is not found in threats and warnings. So in the hope of breaking a few manmade yokes, let's review some of these so-called unforgivable sins.

What are the forgiven sins?

Some say the unforgivable sin is a bad attitude or a lack of reverence or being stubborn and unteachable. This is nonsense. Jesus didn't suffer and die to enter us into a reverence contest. We neither earn points for being quick learners nor get punished for being dimwitted. Attitude is certainly important, as it will affect the way you live, but a poor attitude won't disqualify a saint any more than a good attitude will qualify a sinner.

Others say the unforgivable sin is not loving the Lord with all your heart, soul, and mind. It's putting Sunday football ahead of Jesus. This belief leads naturally to a system of religious scorekeeping. It's the old debits versus the credits chestnut. But God is not counting the number of hours you put into church versus the number of hours you spend kicking a football or whatever it is you do when you're having fun. God invented fun.

The command to love the Lord your God with all your heart, soul, and mind is part of the old law-keeping covenant. Jesus identified it as the greatest commandment "in the law" (see Matthew 22:36–37). You are not under law but grace. Under law you love because you have to, but under grace we love because he first loved us. Law-based love is inferior and contrived. But grace-based love is the real deal.

160

What about willful sin? Is willful sin unforgivable? Well if Jesus can't forgive the sins we've done on purpose, then no one can be saved. Sin is sin. If God kept a record of sin, who could stand (Psalm 130:3)? The good news is not that God has only forgiven some of your sins—the ones you did by accident—but that he has forgiven all your sins for all time.

I've heard some say the unpardonable sins are those we neither repent of nor confess. They seem to forget that Jesus went around forgiving people who neither repented nor confessed nor even asked for forgiveness. They also forget that he forgave us long before we were born. If you think, "I must repent or confess before God will forgive me," you're trusting in dead works. You're putting price tags on grace. The blood of Jesus paid for the sins of an unrepentant world.[1]

What about harboring unforgiveness in our hearts? Didn't Jesus say, "God won't forgive us unless we forgive others"? He did, but only to prove a point to some law-minded Jews. Think about it. If unforgiveness is a sin and God won't forgive us for harboring it, then God himself is sinning by harboring unforgiveness toward us. A sinning God is bad news. But a God who forgives all our sins is good news indeed.[2]

What if I take the Lord's name in vain?

As a child, I knew that saying the name of Jesus in an inappropriate manner was a serious sin. It was something *you just didn't do.* What would happen if you did? I never did it so I never found out. However, I knew people who did and contrary to all expectations, they weren't zapped by lightning. Nor were they taken outside the camp and stoned to death, as happened under the old covenant (see Leviticus 24:15–16).

If you have cursed God or taken the Lord's name in vain, be thankful you live under a new and better covenant. Thank God for Jesus who said:

Anyone who speaks a word against the Son of Man will be forgiven ... (Matthew 12:32a)

You may have cursed God, but he has blessed you. You may have spoken ill of him but he speaks life over you. You may have acted like his enemy, but the good news is God loves his enemies.

But what about the rest of that verse?

> … but anyone who speaks against the Holy Spirit will not be forgiven, either in this age or in the age to come. (Matthew 12:32b)

Here Jesus identifies the one thing that cannot be forgiven, namely, speaking against the Holy Spirit.

What about bad-mouthing the Holy Spirit?

I regularly hear from people who are worried sick that they have committed the unforgivable sin. Some are afraid because of the bad things they have said about God. One man told me,

> I called God an evil spirit. I don't even know why I said it. At the time I didn't know God and now that I do I wouldn't say such things. I've confessed and repented with tears but I'm afraid. Please help.

Others are worried because they have had doubts about God and they fear their doubts have disqualified them from the kingdom. Another man wrote to me and said:

> I was raised a Christian but went through periods of doubt. About a year ago I was watching a video of Christians and atheists debating. For a brief moment I thought, "That makes no sense. God must not be real," and then I said to myself, "I just became an atheist." I began to feel sick and said, "No, I'm a Christian." I went back and forth a few times and felt terrible. I don't know why I said what I did, but I have been worried about it ever since.

These aren't small concerns. A mind that can't find rest in Jesus tends to become hyperactive and prone to breakdown. One illness

I hear about again and again is obsessive compulsive disorder. OCD is an anxiety disorder characterized by hard-to-shake thoughts and repetitive behaviors done in the hope of making the anxieties go away. In a Christian context, anxieties about the unforgivable sin can lead to relentless religious activity, as this story illustrates:

> I have struggled with the issue of unforgivable sin for the last twenty years. I have the most terrible thoughts against the Holy Spirit. I hate these blasphemous and angry thoughts and my inability to stop them. Often my days are filled with confession over these terrible acts. The more I confess, the worse it gets. I was recently diagnosed with OCD.

These are heart-breaking tales, and so unnecessary. They are the bad fruit of bad theology. When you've been told your salvation depends on your ability to say the right things, believe the right things, and never stumble, disaster is inevitable. We are simply not designed to carry such heavy burdens.

We've all said things we regret and done things we wish we hadn't. That's life. The bad news of religion says you must pay for your bad choices, but the good news of grace says Jesus can make all things, including your messes and mistakes, work together for good. He is our great redeemer. He takes broken people and makes them whole. Abraham was a doubter; God turned him into our father in the faith.

If you've said bad things about the Holy Spirit, it probably means you don't know him very well. As for those bad thoughts that sometimes come to mind, don't take ownership of them. As the saying goes, you can't stop the birds flying overhead, but you can stop them building a nest in your hair. You have the mind of Christ, so send those evil thoughts packing.

If you're worried that you have committed the unforgivable sin, don't panic. You haven't crossed some line of no return. How do I know? Because worrying that you have committed the unforgivable sin is a sure sign that you haven't.

So what does it mean to speak against the Holy Spirit?

What is the blasphemy of the Holy Spirit?

> Truly I tell you, people can be forgiven all their sins and every
> slander they utter, but whoever blasphemes against the Holy
> Spirit will never be forgiven … (Mark 3:28–29a)

Although you may fear you have done something unforgivable,
Jesus said that there is only one thing that cannot be forgiven, and
that is speaking against or blaspheming the Holy Spirit. What
does it mean to blaspheme someone? I used to think a blasphemer
was someone who spoke the Lord's name inappropriately, but
that's not quite right. To blaspheme is to slander or to speak
against someone in a manner than injures or discredits their good
name. Here's an example from the Bible:[3]

> Why not say—as some slanderously (*blasphēmeo*) claim that
> we say—"Let us do evil that good may result"? Their condem-
> nation is just! (Romans 3:8)

When people accused Paul of preaching grace as a license to sin,
he said their reports were slanderous or blasphemous. In other
words, their claims were false and injurious to his reputation and
message.

To blaspheme the Holy Spirit is to slander him. It's to speak
against him and his ministry. It's saying no when he says yes. It's
labeling as evil that which he calls good and esteeming that which
he considers detestable.

To understand what it means to speak falsely of the Holy
Spirit, we must discover what is true about him and his ministry.
Here are three things the Holy Spirit does:

> When he has come, he will convict the world … of sin,
> because they do not believe in me. (John 16:8–9, NKJV)

The first thing the Holy Spirit does is seek to convince you that
Jesus is the cure to sin. "In regard to sin, see Jesus." Whether you
are struggling with sin or worried that something you did is
unforgivable, the remedy is the same. Believe in Jesus.

"But Paul, you don't know what I've done." No, you don't know what *Jesus* has done. No matter what you've done or how bad you've been, his death on the cross is the once-and-final solution for all your sin. In him you have full and complete forgiveness for now and ever more.

We discredit Jesus and slander the Holy Spirit by thinking we must act before God will forgive us. "I have to repent and confess to be forgiven." That's back to front. We repent (change our unbelieving minds) and confess (agree with God that Jesus has done it all) because we are forgiven.

Forgiveness is good, but you need more. Forgiveness gets you out but doesn't take you in. To enter the kingdom of heaven, you need the righteousness that exceeds that of the Pharisees (Matthew 5:20).

> When he has come, he will convict the world ... of righteousness, because I go to my Father and you see me no more. (John 16:8,10, NKJV)

The second thing the Holy Spirit does is seek to convince you that the righteousness you need comes as a free gift from God (Romans 1:17).

We discredit Jesus and slander the Holy Spirit by thinking we can make ourselves righteous and pleasing to God. That's the faithless religion of the Pharisee. If you would respond positively to the Holy Spirit, then allow him to persuade you that in Christ you are as righteous as he is. Agree with him and declare, "I am the righteousness of God in Christ Jesus!"

> When he has come, he will convict the world ... of judgment, because the ruler of this world is judged. (John 16:8, 11, NKJV)

The third aspect of the Holy Spirit's ministry is seeking to convince you that the prince of this world stands condemned. You are not condemned; Satan is. If you are responsive to the Holy Spirit's conviction, you will declare, "There is now no condemnation for me who is in Christ Jesus!" You will ask with wonder, "If God is for me, who can be against me?" (Romans 8:1, 31).

We discredit Jesus and slander the Holy Spirit by thinking we will be judged as sinners or that God punishes us for our mistakes. That's dismissing the cross. It's saying Jesus *hasn't* carried the sin of the world and our sins *haven't* been removed as far as the east is from the west.

What is the blasphemy of the Holy Spirit? It is refusing to believe what the Holy Spirit says about Jesus. It's scorning the grace of God that qualifies us and it's trampling the Son of God underfoot. In a word, it is unbelief. It's speaking against the Holy Spirit by saying, "Jesus' work remains unfinished, and I remain unforgiven, unrighteous, and under condemnation."

Perhaps you have said something like this. Perhaps you have done all the things I've just mentioned. You've religiously confessed your sins because you thought God wouldn't forgive you if you didn't. Or perhaps you've worked hard to make yourself righteous because you didn't know the righteousness that comes by grace. Perhaps you have spoken against the Holy Spirit again and again. Does this mean you can never be saved? Does this mean you have committed an eternal sin?

What is the eternal sin?

> But whoever blasphemes against the Holy Spirit will never be forgiven; he is guilty of an eternal sin. (Mark 3:29)

In a sense, there is no such thing as an eternal sin. Every sin was forgiven or carried away at the cross. To suggest Jesus missed one sin, as some translations do, is to imply his work was less than perfect.

Jesus is not saying your sins won't be forgiven—they already have been. He's saying you'll never experience his forgiveness if you resist the Holy Spirit. You'll never walk in grace if you resist the Spirit of grace.

We can resist grace two ways: by hardening our hearts to God and saying, "I don't need you," or by trusting the religious spirit that says, "I can make it on my own." Both attitudes are fatal.

You need to know that the Holy Spirit is the best friend you've got. He is the most powerful being in the universe and every day he will seek to point you towards Jesus. When you sin, he will reassure you that you are forgiven. When you stumble, he will tell you that in Christ you are as righteous as ever. And when condemnation comes, he will remind you that your Father is for you and nothing can separate you from his love.

What is your part in this? It is to speak *with* the Holy Spirit and not against him. It is to agree with God and not deny him. It is to thank Jesus and not supplant him. If you call Jesus "Lord," then be at peace, for in him you are eternally safe and secure and forgiven indeed!

Who is a blasphemer?

A man called Charles wrote to me because he thought he had committed the unforgivable sin. "I heard someone speaking in tongues and said, 'That person is demon possessed.'" Charles was worried because he had acted like the Pharisees, who ascribed to the devil the work of the Spirit.

The Pharisees saw Jesus casting out demons and said, "By the prince of demons he is driving out demons" (Mark 3:22). Jesus responded by warning them not to blaspheme the Holy Spirit. But the Pharisees' problem was not that they were confused about Jesus' source of power. Their problem was they were resistant to the gospel Jesus was demonstrating right before their eyes.

A demon-possessed man who was blind and mute was brought to the Lord. Jesus drove out the demon so that the man could talk and see. When the Pharisees said, "This is the devil's work," Jesus didn't respond with, "You blasphemers. You'll never be forgiven for saying that!" He said, "Are you nuts? If Satan were driving out Satan, there wouldn't be any Satan left" (see Matthew 12:26, MSG).

I have seen supernatural activity which some Christians attributed to God and others to the devil. They can't both be right. Because I preach the gospel of grace, some Christians have called me a servant of the Lord, while others have said I am an instrument of Satan. Again, they can't both be right. From time to time, sincere believers are spectacularly wrong about what God is doing among them. They repeat the mistake of the Pharisees. But

167

that doesn't mean they have committed the unforgivable sin. It just means they are confused.

What does a blasphemer look like? Religion paints a picture of a blasphemer as someone who is belligerent or foul-mouthed. But a blasphemer may look respectable, like a Pharisee. The distinguishing characteristic of a blasphemer is not that they are confused, like Charles. It's that they call God a liar.

> If we have faith in God's Son, we have believed what God has said. But if we don't believe what God has said about his Son, it is the same as calling God a liar. (1 John 5:10, CEV)

By his own admission the apostle Paul "was once a blasphemer and a persecutor and a violent man" (1 Timothy 1:13). As a Pharisee, Paul resisted the Holy Spirit and refused to believe his testimony about Jesus. By speaking against the Holy Spirit Paul committed the unforgivable sin. He essentially said "God is a liar." But God didn't write him off. He kept pouring out his grace until one day Paul saw the light. This shows us that no one is beyond the reach of grace, not even violent blasphemers like Paul.

This is good news for those like Søren Kierkegaard who worry they have committed the unforgivable sin. If you are worried, get your eyes off yourself and your sin and look to Jesus. Stop resisting the Spirit of grace and allow him to persuade you that the love of God is greater than all your sin—your unconfessed sin, your willful sin, your habitual sin—even those sins you thought were unforgivable.

I wish I could go back to nineteenth-century Copenhagen, find the gloomy Dane, and tell him the good news. "Søren, all your sins have been forgiven. God holds nothing against you." The gospel is the cure for gloominess. The gospel is the joyful declaration that God loves the stubborn and the disrespectful. He even loves blasphemers.

16. Once Saved, Always Saved?

I have a beard, so you may find this hard to believe, but I shave every day. Most men do. I understand many women also shave regularly. Perhaps you were shaved at one time, but that doesn't mean you are shaved now. You have to work to stay shaved. You may profess a belief in shaving, but faith without regular works of shaving shaves no one.

Shaving is a tricky business. You need to hold fast when you shave. You have to work out your shaving with fear and trembling because only he who shaves firm to the end will be shaved.

I'm smiling as I write this. Why? Because apparently being shaved and being *saved* have much in common. You have to work hard at both of them. At least that's what some people think.

For those of you who have no idea what I'm talking about, I'm having a gentle dig at those who ridicule the phrase, "Once saved, always saved." Why anyone would want to scorn the believer's security is beyond me. It's like mocking marriage.

Your security in Christ is a big deal. It's something to treasure, not scorn.

Since childhood I have known that I am secure in my Father's love—he holds me, he keeps me, and he will never let me go. But many are not secure. They've been told they have to abide, continue, hold fast to the end, overcome, obey, endure, and otherwise do things to stay saved. Naturally, this unsettles them. *What if I don't do what God expects of me? What if I stumble at the last hurdle? What then?*

If this is you, then this chapter, and the three that follow ought to help. We're going to look at some of the key scriptures on the subject of your security. After we unpack these scriptures in light of who Christ is and what he has done for us, you're going to be so blessed. You're going to want to shout and thank Jesus from the rooftops.

But before we jump in, let's take a moment to polish our spectacles and check for cracks in the lenses.

What are the blind spots of the insecure?

What you look through determines what you see. If you look at the world through a cracked lens, everything will appear fuzzy and distorted. Similarly, if you have a distorted view of God, everything you read will be filtered through your distortion.

Taking that one step further, if you are insecure and uncertain about your position in Christ, then parts of the Bible will appear to support your prior notions of insecurity.

I appreciate this works both ways. If I come to the Bible secure in my Father's love, then everything I read will appear to confirm my prior notions of security. So how do we decide which perspective is correct? The only way is to filter the written word through the Living Word — who Jesus is and what he has done.

I'm not claiming to be the final authority on how to interpret scripture. Every one of us has blind spots and we're all learning. But may I humbly suggest that if you are insecure about your salvation, your vision may be obscured by one of three blind spots.

Blind spot #1: The insecure don't see God as their Father
Jesus came to reveal God our Father and it is this revelation that makes the new covenant new. And this is what makes a Christian a Christian — we have received the Spirit of sonship. We are God's children. We have been adopted in and we will never be adopted out. But the insecure don't see it. At best, God is a generic Father of humanity, but he's certainly not Daddy. He's more like a judge or employer who grades us on our performance.

Lacking the confidence that comes from knowing the Father's love, the insecure filter his words through an orphan's anxieties. Their survival instincts keep them from fully trusting his promises.

They may have enough faith to be saved but not enough to rest. They have to stay vigilant lest they drift away.

Blind spot #2: The insecure don't fully appreciate the cross
The insecure may know Jesus died for them but they don't know that his death ended the old system of rule-keeping. Consequently, they interpret new covenant promises as old covenant threats.

A classic example is the commands of Jesus which the insecure read as *instructions that must be obeyed if you want to stay saved* (see chapter 14). Other examples include the exhortations to continue in the faith (chapter 18) and endure to the end (chapter 9). When these are read as conditions for maintaining salvation, a cross-shaped blind spot is revealed.

Blind spot #3. The insecure don't see salvation as a Person
The insecure treat the gift of salvation as though it comes in a box. If you don't hold on to it you could lose it. Like your car keys, you can misplace your salvation if you're not careful.

Salvation is not a box; it's a Person. It is Christ living in you. "Christ is your life" (Colossians 3:4). It's always a good idea to hold onto Jesus, but even if you don't he still holds on to you, and the good news is he will never let you go (John 10:28).

Whose promises are you standing on?

Have you ever broken a promise or failed to keep your word? You probably have. Now you know why some people are worried they may fail God. They made a commitment to follow the Lord, but the pattern of their lives reveals a consistent inability to deliver. They have good days when they confidently declare, "Lord, I will serve you with all of my heart." But then they have bad days when they feel like a failure. "Lord, I messed up." One week they're up, the next they're down. One Sunday they're making promises; the next they are apologizing for breaking them. It's an endless cycle.

The problem is they are standing on the brittle promises they've made to God when they ought to be standing on the rock-solid promises he's made to us. They are focusing on their own "I wills" rather than the eternal "He wills" declared in scripture.

Ask them if they have any assurance of salvation and the honest ones reply, "I don't know. I hope so, but I'm not certain." Their uncertainty reveals the shakiness of their manmade foundations.

Uncertainty is a faith-killer. If you are uncertain about what God has said, how will you be able to stand on his promises? If you don't settle this issue of eternal security in your heart, you'll always wonder whether you have done enough to qualify.

Uncertainty regarding the promises of God is actually unbelief. If you are uncertain and in doubt, know that I write so that you might repent (change your unbelieving mind) and believe the good news. I write so that you might trust Jesus to finish what he started.

If I could show you just one promise from the Lord that guaranteed your eternal security, would you quit fretting? Would you stop heeding the misgivings of the muddled and instead trust in the Rock of your salvation? Would one bankable promise from the Faithful One do it for you? Well, here's one:

> He also will keep you firm to the end, so that you will be blameless on the day of our Lord Jesus Christ. God is faithful who has called you into fellowship with his Son, Jesus Christ our Lord. (1 Corinthians 1:8–9)

This scripture is the atom bomb that obliterates the doubts of the insecure. If you struggle with doubt and uncertainty, you should frame this verse. It will remind you that salvation is not about your faithfulness, but his and "God is faithful."

It is the nature of the flesh to grasp and strive and say, "I will," but it is the nature of faith to rest and trust and say, "He will." That's the hope-filled message Paul is preaching here: "He will ... so that you will ..."

Let's look at that passage again, this time in the Message Bible:

> The evidence of Christ has been clearly verified in your lives. Just think—you don't need a thing, you've got it all! ... And not only that, but God himself is right alongside to keep you steady and on track until things are all wrapped up by Jesus. God, who got you started in this spiritual adventure, shares with us the life of his Son and our Master Jesus. He will never give up on you. Never forget that. (1 Corinthians 1:6–9, MSG)

You may give up on God, but he will never give up on you, and that's what counts.

And let's not forget who Paul was writing to either. He's addressing the Corinthians, folks who were unlikely to win big at the Good Christian Awards. The Corinthian church was a scandal, yet Paul looks at these substandard saints, sees God's fingerprints all over them, and speaks confidently of their future. "Our hope for you is firm" (2 Corinthians 1:7).

Who called you into fellowship with Christ? God. Who will keep you strong to the end so that you will be blameless on that day? God. Who is faithful? God. It's not about you but him.

Here's another promise you can stand on:

> Now it is God who makes both us and you stand firm in Christ. He anointed us, set his seal of ownership on us, and put his Spirit in our hearts as a deposit, guaranteeing what is to come. (2 Corinthians 1:21–22)

The word *guarantee* means a down payment or pledge, "given in advance as security for the rest."[1] So either God has nothing but more good stuff planned for you — guaranteed! — or he is a liar.

What does God say about my future?

I said one promise from the Lord should be enough, and I've given you two. Just to settle matters once and for all, here are seven more promises from your heavenly Father that speak directly to your eternal security. Write them on your heart and take them to the bank because they are gold.

For a Christian to lose their salvation and be expelled from the kingdom...

1. God would have to forsake us, when he said he wouldn't (Hebrews 13:5).
2. God would have to cast us out, when he said he wouldn't (John 6:37).
3. God would have to condemn us, when he said he wouldn't (Romans 8:1, 34).
4. God would have to withdraw his Spirit, when he said he wouldn't (John 14:16–17).

173

5. God would have to remember our sins, when he said he wouldn't (Jeremiah 31:34, Hebrews 10:17).
6. God would have to forget that we are his children, when he said he wouldn't (Isaiah 49:15).
7. God would have to blot our names out of the book of life, when he said he wouldn't (Revelation 3:5).

Isn't this good news? Come on. This is the best news in the world! I know these promises aren't widely proclaimed, but they should be. God's promises, which are embodied in Jesus, are meant to be a sure foundation for your times (Isaiah 33:6).

"Paul, I don't quite get this. Are you saying we don't need to respond to Jesus?" No, you definitely need to respond. But the response God is looking for is child-like faith, not a lifetime of flawless Christian performance. Faith is a rest. Faith is saying, "I distrust myself; I trust Jesus. He has done it all."

> For no matter how many promises God has made, they are "Yes" in Christ. (2 Corinthians 1:20a)

If you are trying to deliver on promises you have made to God, you will be anxious and fruitless. You'll lie awake wondering if you have done enough to qualify. The cure for your insecurity is Jesus. He is the emphatic "Yes!" to all of God's promises.

Does God use correction fluid?

The promises of God ought to be an anchor for your soul, but when you don't know God as your Father or you haven't seen the finished work of the cross, unbelief can be hard to shake. In the minds of the anxious these promises can actually become threats. Consider this promise from Jesus:

> He who overcomes shall be clothed in white garments, and I will not blot out his name from the Book of Life; but I will confess his name before my Father and before his angels. (Revelation 3:5, NKJV)

Some Christians read this and worry that Jesus will do the very thing he promised not to do. They fear he will blot out their names from the Lamb's Book of Life. And why would he do that? Because we mess up and make mistakes. "If I don't overcome in the trials of life, I'm going to be blotted out. I'll be disqualified from the kingdom."

Why do they read it this way? Because they have an old covenant mindset that says, "I'm safe as long as I don't sin."

> The Lord replied to Moses, "Whoever has sinned against me I will blot out of my book." (Exodus 32:33)

Under the old covenant, your performance mattered a great deal. You were safe if you were good but lost if you weren't. Naturally this made people anxious and insecure. *What if I stumble? What if I fall? God will blot me out of his book!*

But we don't live under that old, sin-conscious covenant. We live under the new and better covenant of God's grace. Under grace, your performance affects your standing not one bit. Jesus did it all. We are not blessed because we are faithful, but because he is faithful.

If you are worried about getting your name blotted out, you are reading a new covenant promise through an old covenant lens. Read the words of Jesus again. "I will never blot out his name." Never means *never*. It's meant to be good news. It's meant to give you peace and comfort. It's meant to make you smile.

"But Paul, it's a promise with conditions. It only applies to those who overcome." Don't you see? In the new covenant, Jesus fulfills all the conditions on your behalf. In him you have already overcome the world (John 16:33). There is no overcoming outside of Jesus.

"Paul, you're taking this out of context. Jesus has just warned those in Sardis that they need to repent or they will be in trouble." Actually Jesus identifies two groups of people in Sardis. There was a group that remained dead in sins and needed to get saved and another group dressed in white (see Revelation 3:1–4). Jesus is distinguishing those who trust him from those who don't. The promises of God are not for those who reject him. They're for those who trust him. Have you received the grace of God that comes through Jesus? Then the promise is for you.

"It can't be that simple. If Jesus is offering a carrot, there must be a stick. If he's saying we can go in, there must be a chance we can go out." Now there's a thought. It's like Jesus is sitting in heaven with a pen in one hand and a bottle of correction fluid in the other. Get saved, name goes in. Fail a test, name goes out. Recommit your life to God, name goes back in. With all the recommitments going on, you'd think Jesus was in danger of repetitive stress injury.

God knows you better than you know yourself. When he added your name to his book he knew everything you had done and everything you would do. There is nothing you can do that will surprise him, nothing that would cause him to shake his head with disappointment and say, "I made a mistake adopting that one." God doesn't make mistakes. When he added you to his book it was for all eternity.

In the new covenant there is only one thing that God promises to blot out, and it's not your name—it's your sins:

> I, even I, am he who blots out your transgressions, for my own sake, and remembers your sins no more. (Isaiah 43:25)

God promised to blot out all your sins and he did that already. If your sins have been blotted out, then your name cannot be. This was good news for the saints in Sardis, and it's good news for us today.

What about this tricky scripture?

"But Paul, what about all those scriptures that say we have to hold fast, continue, and endure to the end?"[2]

We'll to get to some of those scriptures in the coming chapters, but let me put your mind at rest right now. Do you have a need to hold fast? Do you have a need to continue and endure? Do you have a need to overcome, obey, avoid sin, be holy, and persevere? Yes, we all have these needs. But look at this ...

My God will meet all your needs according to the riches of his glory in Christ Jesus. (Philippians 4:19)

How many of your needs will God meet? All of them. How many of your needs must you supply to stay qualified for the kingdom? None of them. Your part is to receive by faith what God has already provided in Christ Jesus. Your part is to say, "Thank you Jesus!" and then abide in that place of grateful trust.

Anything and everything that needs to be done to see you safe to the end, will be done by him. Trust him. The one who "began a good work in you will carry it on to completion" (Philippians 1:6). (Another promise.) Salvation is not from yourself, it is the gift of God (Ephesians 2:8), and his gifts are irrevocable (Romans 11:29). (Two more promises!)

No doubt there will be some who say I am presenting an unbalanced view, that I have left out important bits of the Bible. What they really mean, though, is God is a mealy-mouthed mincer of words who doesn't say what he means or mean what he says. I disagree. Through the death and resurrection of his Son, God shouts to the human race, "I am for you and I will do whatever it takes to win you back to myself!" I believe him. I put no confidence in my promises to him but choose to stand on his promises to us. I encourage you to do likewise.

Saint, you are one with the Lord. His future is your future. Since Jesus isn't going to lose his salvation and go to hell, it can't happen to you. You may fall asleep on the job, but the one who watches over you never slumbers (Psalm 121:3–4). Be confident. Be secure. Be at peace.

17. Is the Christian Race a Marathon?

The 135-mile Badwater Ultramarathon is known as the world's toughest foot race. It is run in Death Valley in 130-degree summer heat, and there is almost no shade. The course is so hot that runners who don't stick to the straight and narrow of the painted white lines can find their sneakers melting into the tarmac. Not only is it hot and long, it's uphill. The course covers three mountain ranges, ascending a cumulative total of 13,000 feet.

Dean Karnazes, who won the race in 2004, has said, "No matter how many times I attempt the Badwater Ultramarathon, it never seems to get any easier." It is the mother of all endurance races.[1]

The New Testament writers likened Christianity to a race.[2] But what kind of race is it? Is the Christian race like the Badwater Ultra? Is it something to be endured rather than enjoyed? And do only those who endure to the end qualify for the kingdom?

You might think so to read verses such as these: "We must go through many hardships to enter the kingdom of God" (Acts 14:22). "If we endure, we will also reign with him" (2 Timothy 2:12). "We have come to share in Christ if we hold firmly till the end the confidence we had at first" (Hebrews 3:14). "Be faithful, even to the point of death, and I will give you the crown of life" (Revelation 2:10).

What are we to make of these scriptures? Read around and you will find there are two views on endurance. The first says salvation is indeed conditional on enduring. If you don't endure to the end you're lost forever. The second says enduring to the end proves you are saved. If you didn't endure, you weren't saved to begin with. I have problems with both views.

Is salvation conditional on your endurance?

My problem with the first view is that it contradicts the many promises of God regarding our eternal salvation (see chapter 16). It's a simple choice: Either God keeps us strong to the end (like he promised) or he doesn't. Either God will make us stand firm in Christ (like he said) or he won't.[3]

179

Here's the bad news: If our salvation depends on us, then we're not saved by his grace but our enduring performance. And if *that* were true, God is a liar, Jesus is a failure, and the Holy Spirit has not made his permanent home in us.

But the good news declares that Jesus is both the author *and* the perfecter of your faith. Jesus does good work and he never leaves a job unfinished. You can trust him to complete the good work he started in you.

Does enduring merely prove you were saved all along?

My problem with the second view — that enduring proves you were saved — is that it's useless. Since you won't know until the end whether you have endured or not, how can you have any assurance that you are saved today? You can't. Instead of standing secure on the promises of God, you'll be unstable, tossed to and fro by every wind of teaching. You'll be easy prey for the insurance agents of dead religion. And your uncertainty will cause you to be fearful of sin and intolerant of other people's mistakes. Consider the following conversation:

Stan: "Did you hear that Paul Ellis stumbled in sin? Such a great man of God too — who would've thought it?"

Jan: "Well that just proves Paul was never saved after all. Boy, were we fooled."

Dan: "Oh well, live and learn. Since it's impossible for those who have once been enlightened to be brought back to the place of repentance, we won't bother praying for him or calling him up to encourage him. He's a write-off. I can't believe we wasted all that time on him."

Some Christians are so scared of sin in the camp that when a brother sins, if he doesn't leave the camp, they just move the camp!

Why are there so many scriptures on endurance?

The scriptures on endurance are not there to instill you with fear and uncertainty but to inspire you to trust the One who said this:

> I have told you these things, so that in me you may have peace. In this world you will have trouble. But take heart! I have overcome the world. (John 16:33)

At first glance, these words of Jesus are a real head-scratcher. *Jesus says I will have trouble, but he has overcome the world. How is this good news for me? I'm not Jesus.*

Jesus is saying, "Life is one big endurance race, but take heart, I've already won it." *Again, Lord, how is this good news?* It is good news indeed for those who are *in Christ*.

Look again at Jesus' words: "I have told you these things, so that *in me* you may have peace." The Christian race is a marathon, but for those of us *in Christ*, the race begins at the finish line. Indeed, it begins on the winners' podium, for when you were placed into Christ, you were placed into the race winner.

Jesus said, "I have overcome the world." What did he mean by that? He meant the devil couldn't tempt him, the law-lovers couldn't silence him, Pilate couldn't fault him, death couldn't keep him, and the grave couldn't hold him. Jesus is the ultimate overcomer. Look up the word *overcomer* in the dictionary and you'll find a picture of Jesus.

Again, you might ask, "That's all very fine for Jesus. But what about me? When Jesus challenges me to be an overcomer, what does he mean?" Here is your answer:

> You, dear children, are from God and have overcome them, because the One who is in you is greater than the one who is in the world. (1 John 4:4)

Overcoming is not about jumping through hoops and impressing God with your overcoming performance. It's about depending on *the* Overcomer who lives in you.

For everyone born of God overcomes the world. This is the victory that has overcome the world, even our faith. Who is it that overcomes the world? Only the one who believes that Jesus is the Son of God. (1 John 5:4–5)

Are you born of God? Do you believe Jesus is the Son of God? If so, then the Overcomer lives in you. His overcoming nature is your new nature. It's who you truly are.

Are you an elephant or a turtle?

Think of it like this. If your mother was an elephant and your father was an elephant, then you can't help but be an elephant. The world may tell you that you are a turtle, and you may even speak turtle, but at best you will only ever be an elephant doing impressions. He who has big ears, let him hear!

When you came to Christ he made you a new creation. He gave you his mighty overcoming Spirit, and you are now an overcomer by nature. You may not feel like an overcomer. You may feel like a turtle. But you are an overcomer nonetheless. If you choose to act like a victim or a loser or anything other than an overcomer, you are acting contrary to your Christ-given nature. You are not walking in your true identity.

Just as an elephant is not an elephant because he acts like an elephant, neither are you an overcomer because you overcome from time to time. That's back to front. You act like an overcomer because in Christ you *are* an overcomer. It's a fact.

As it is written: "For your sake we face death all day long; we are considered as sheep to be slaughtered." No, in all these things we are more than conquerors through him who loved us. (Romans 8:36–37)

From a worldly point of view you may not look like an overcomer. You may appear to be a worn out, beat up, raggedy ol' saint with problems left and right. The circumstances of your life may be telling you that you are not an overcomer. Ignore those faithless voices. Don't listen to them. They don't have all the facts. They are speaking from an earthly reality. But we are from God and he says we are more than conquerors through Christ, who loved us. Believe what your Father says about you.

Overcomers endure. It's in their nature to outlast the opposition. The One who is in you is greater than the one who opposes you. Victory is inevitable, for Jesus *always* wins.

How can I endure the unendurable?

From time to time you will have a great need for endurance. The good news is that God has promised to supply that need, along with all your other needs, according to his riches in glory by Christ Jesus (Philippians 4:19).

There will be times in your life when your natural reserves of endurance, patience and perseverance will run out. You'll be running on empty. You'll be at the end of your rope and past your breaking point.

The good news is Jesus has bucketloads of endurance to share with you. Since he has already endured and since his love endures all things, his supply will never run out. Your part is to receive what he provides.

But there's a problem. You won't receive for as long as you're trying to make it on your own. If you think you can manufacture endurance through discipline or intestinal fortitude, you are setting yourself up for disaster. Life is bigger than you and me. The trials you face will eventually break you, no matter how strong your resolve. The sooner you quit trying to survive through grit and determination, the sooner you will be able to tap into your Father's abundant supply of grace.

Can you imagine what it must've been like to be rounded up with other believers and sent to the Roman circus to face the lions? Can you imagine waiting in the holding cell for your turn to be torn and devoured? I can tell you that in my natural strength I would have been climbing the walls trying to get out. Or perhaps I would have been curled up in the fetal position, overcome with fear.

Yet when you read about the first-century Christians you learn that some actually *volunteered* for the circus. Like Paul, they considered it an honor to share a martyr's death with the Lord. In other words, when the pressure came they found within themselves the fire-hardened steel of Christ's endurance, and it gave them supernatural courage.

It's the same today. I have known Chinese pastors who have thought going to prison to be a small thing. If you know anything about Chinese prisons you'll know that's not a normal reaction. It is not natural to be untroubled by such things, and yet they are. They endure the unendurable because Christ the Overcomer empowers them.

> Consider it pure joy, my brothers and sisters, whenever you face trials of many kinds, because you know that the testing of your faith produces perseverance. Let perseverance finish its work so that you may be mature and complete, not lacking anything. (James 1:2–4)

In Christ you lack nothing, but you won't know you lack nothing until you've been tested by the trials of life. It is only when you have gone past breaking point and found God waiting, strong, and smiling that you begin to realize that when you are weak, you can be strong indeed.

It is not a joyful thing to be persecuted. The joy comes in discovering that the faith God has put in you is worth more than gold.

> In all this you greatly rejoice, though now for a little while you may have had to suffer grief in all kinds of trials. These have come so that the proven genuineness of your faith—of greater worth than gold, which perishes even though refined by fire—may result in praise, glory and honor when Jesus Christ is revealed. (1 Peter 1:6–7)

The trials of life are not to see whether we can manufacture the Right Stuff for Jesus, for we can't manufacture faith at all. Faith is a gift from God. The purpose of life's trials is to prove to you that God's gifts are awesome.

What about these scriptures on endurance?

> We must go through many hardships to enter the kingdom of God. (Acts 14:22b)

Paul is not saying we have to jump through hardship hoops to qualify for the kingdom—that's the pagan doctrine of asceticism that Paul expressly rejected (see Colossians 2:20–23). Rather, he's paraphrasing what Jesus said about having troubles in this world. He's saying, "We Christians go through trials and tribulations from time to time." And he should know. Just five verses earlier Paul was stoned and left for dead!

> Here is a trustworthy saying: If we died with him, we will also live with him; if we endure, we will also reign with him. If we disown him, he will also disown us; if we are faithless, he remains faithful, for he cannot disown himself. (2 Timothy 2:11–13)

The first part is referring to believers. Who has died with Christ but those who identify with his death and resurrection? Jesus tasted death for everyone. He died for the whole world. But his representative death only benefits those who wish to be represented.[4]

The Christian life begins at death. This is what makes the gospel unique. Every manmade religion preaches self-denial and dying to self, but the gospel simply declares, "You died." And we died so that Christ might live through us. This is the miracle of new life. "I no longer live, but Christ lives in me" (Galatians 2:20).

"But wait," says Paul. "There's more. There's a whole other part to this trustworthy saying. We don't merely live, we also endure and reign." This new life we have in Christ is a new kind of life characterized by supernatural endurance and reigning in all things.

If Paul had said, "Work hard and endure and maybe you will get to reign," that would be nothing special or trustworthy. That's how the world works. But verse 12 follows right after verse 11. Paul is describing the life we have in union with the One who already overcame, already endured, and now reigns. "This life we have in Christ is an enduring and reigning life," says Paul. "It's like nothing on earth."

Do you see? Paul is giving us a three-part punchline. He's saying, "You know you died with Christ, right?" *Yes, Paul, I know.* "Well do you also know that you will live with Christ?" *Sure, Paul, in eternity.* "No, not just in eternity but here and now. You will endure *here*. You will reign in life *here*. This is a trustworthy saying that deserves your full acceptance." *Oh, I didn't know that Paul. That's really good news!*

Many Christians are looking forward to a future life with Christ but they are not ruling and reigning with him here and now. They don't know they can. They've been told life is one big test and maybe, if they are careful, they'll get a crown at the end. This brings us to the second part of the passage: "If we disown him, he will also disown us."

What if I disown Jesus?

An insecure believer worries, *What if I disown Jesus in a moment of weakness?* Paul is not talking about this. He is describing those who reject Christ and will one day reap the consequences of their choice. There's no grace for the faithless because the faithless will not receive it.

Paul's words are a warning for the ungodly but they should not unsettle you. We who have acknowledged Christ before others cannot unacknowledge him. We who have been born again cannot be unborn. If you were to deny him, as Peter did three times, Jesus won't disown you, for he cannot disown himself.

> We have come to share in Christ, if indeed we hold our original conviction firmly to the very end. (Hebrews 3:14)

This verse has been used to sow fear into the minds of the insecure. "God got you started, but now it's up to you to finish, so don't screw this up." That's not good news. In fact, it's idolatrous slander. It promotes the carnal idea that heaven will be populated by spiritual Sinatras singing, "I did it my way." That's not going to happen. It's *his* way or the high way. There is no other way.

If Hebrews 3 were saying it's up to us to finish what God started, it would be contradicting Hebrews 12, which says Jesus is the author and finisher of our faith.

The author of Hebrews is not preaching a salvation that is conditional on our perseverance. He's saying, "We have been made partakers of Christ—it's done—but we won't experience the benefits of our union unless we hold firmly to the confidence we had when we started out." He's not threatening us; he's encouraging us to continue as we started—by faith.

> Blessed is the man who endures temptation; for when he has been approved, he will receive the crown of life which the Lord has promised to those who love him. (James 1:12, NKJV)

Here's the insecure view: "If you succumb to temptation and sin, you'll be rejected and won't receive a crown of life." This is not good news.

How are we to read James through the lens of the cross? A good place to start is to ask, "Who is the man that endured and has been approved?" It is Jesus. It is also the one who is *with him* and *in him*. No one outside of Christ is going to pass muster on that day, and no one in Christ is going to be rejected. We are tested and approved *in Christ*.

The trials of life are not to test our suitability for the kingdom but to reveal the genuineness of the faith God has given us. This is why we're blessed and approved and crown-worthy—not because we are resilient but because God is gracious and his gifts are good.

> Be faithful until death, and I will give you the crown of life. (Revelation 2:10b, NKJV)

Here is another verse that seems to link the believer's crown to the believer's faithfulness. The insecure implication is that if you prove unfaithful, you won't get a crown. It's actually worse if you know the back-story. Jesus is speaking to the church in Smyrna. He's just told them that some of their number will be imprisoned, tortured, and executed. If you are insecure that really ought to mess with your head. You may think, *Getting into heaven's tougher than getting into the Navy Seals. Only the strongest make it. I haven't got a chance.*

I hope by now you realize that Jesus is saying nothing of the kind. Here is my paraphrase of his words to the saints in Smyrna:

> Some of you are going to be persecuted on my account and some of you will even die. Don't be afraid but fix your eyes on me. I've been through it all and I have overcome the world. Trust me. We're going to go through this trial together, and you're going to be amazed at how well your God-given faith bears up under pressure. This test will only be for a short time and then we will meet face to face. I can't wait to see you and hug you and give you your crown.

Jesus is such a wonderful encourager. He knows that the only way we can get through life's trials is if we keep our eyes firmly on him.

What is it that helps us overcome the world? It is not our grit, our resolve, or anything to do with our flesh. It is trusting in Jesus. It is facing our trials with our eyes fixed on the One who speaks to storms. It is looking beyond the giants and seeing the King who towers above all. It is betting on Jesus, who is greater than the world.

18. What Does It Mean to Continue in the Faith?

Read the Bible with an old covenant mindset, and you may be confused by those scriptures urging us to "continue in the faith" or "continue in the grace of God." Under the old law covenant, continuing was the difference between life and death. If you didn't continue to keep the law day in and day out, you were doomed.

Just look what happened to Achan. He helped himself to some war booty and was executed for violating God's command. Then there was Uzzah, who tried to steady the Ark of the Covenant and got struck down for his efforts.[1]

That's the problem with living under the law. If you keep the law six days a week but break it on the seventh, you won't get a round of applause for getting it mostly right. You won't even get partial credit, for the law is an all-or-nothing proposition. Break one command one time and you're a law-breaker, guilty of breaking the whole shebang. Live under the law and your motto could be, "Continue or be cursed."

> For all who rely on the works of the law are under a curse, as it is written: "Cursed is everyone who does not continue to do everything written in the Book of the Law." (Galatians 3:10)

In the old covenant, people were kept on the straight and narrow through their fear of being cursed. Today, many live with the same fear. They worry that if they don't continue to pray, continue to fast, continue to give, and meet together, they will be cursed. Or they won't be blessed, which is about the same thing.

If this is you, here is the good news: Jesus died to set us free from the curse of the law. He died to liberate us from the treadmill of ceaseless effort and rule-keeping.

Make no mistake, the old covenant emphasis on continuing is a cursed way to live. It's cursed because it's beyond us. We can't attain it. None of us apart from Jesus is capable of delivering a flawless performance. All of us fall short of the required standard. This is what makes the gospel of grace such good news. In Christ, we are credited with *his* flawless performance. The test has been taken, and in him we have passed with flying colors. In Christ we are judged righteous and holy and blessed for eternity.

With the curse of the law behind us and the grace of God before us, we can now look at those New Testament scriptures exhorting us to continue.

How do I continue in the faith?

> But now he has reconciled you by Christ's physical body through death to present you holy in his sight, without blemish and free from accusation — if you continue in your faith, established and firm, and do not move from the hope held out in the gospel. (Colossians 1:22–23a)

This scripture used to be a splinter in my mind. I didn't know what to make of it. It seems to say that our salvation is conditional on continuing in the faith and that if you stop continuing you'll be cut off. Jesus will divorce you.

This was jarring to me. *How could that happen?* I could not conceive of ever rejecting Jesus, but if the unthinkable did happen, I could not conceive of him rejecting me. It just didn't seem possible. But there it is in black and white: "If you continue in the faith." Clearly something bad will happen if you don't, otherwise Paul would not have mentioned it.

Then one day the scales fell off. I began to see that Paul was not making threats so much as exhorting us to remain in the secure place of Christ's love.

To continue in the faith simply means, "keep trusting Jesus." Paul explains this a few verses later:

> So then, just as you received Christ Jesus as Lord, continue to live your lives in him … (Colossians 2:6)

How did you receive him? By faith. How should you continue to live in him? By faith, "rooted and built up in him, strengthened in the faith as you were taught, and overflowing with thankfulness" (Colossians 2:7). It's faith from first to last.

The problem is we may start out with faith then drift towards unbelief. An attitude of gratitude gets traded for one of fear and insecurity. This can happen when we buy into mixed-up messages like these: "You have to prove your repentance with your deeds, so get busy for Jesus." "Every tree that doesn't produce fruit will be chopped down, so start producing." "Those who are lukewarm are spewed out, so get hot for the Lord."

Now instead of trusting Jesus to finish what he started, the worried believer begins to panic. He thinks, *I don't want to get spewed out, so I had better do something about it.*

This is precisely what was happening to the Colossians. They were falling from the high place of unmerited favor to the low place of human effort. They were falling for the mother of all lies.

What is the mother of all lies?

Many believers have an unhealthy fear of sin. They imagine sin to be this monster lurking outside the church, seeking to devour wayward Christians. But sin is not the true monster. The real danger for the spirit-filled believer is walking after the flesh. It's relying on our natural understanding instead of trusting Jesus. Walking after the flesh can certainly lead to sin because anything that is not of faith is sin. But it may not be the sort of sin you were warned about in youth group.

The Colossian Christians weren't what we would call sinners. They weren't fooling around like the Corinthians. They weren't driving their chariots drunk or downloading naughty pictures off the Internet. Yet according to Paul, they were on a downward spiral. They were in danger of losing their freedom in Christ. This is why he says:

> See to it that no one takes you captive through hollow and deceptive philosophy, which depends on human tradition and the elemental spiritual forces of this world rather than on Christ. (Colossians 2:8)

What is hollow and deceptive philosophy? It's any message that puts the emphasis on you instead of Christ. It's anything that says you need to do stuff to get God to bless you. Buy into such a message and you will lose the freedom you have in Christ. You'll tie yourself up in knots trying to obtain what you already possess. You'll no longer be continuing in faith but unbelief.

Nothing will stop you trusting in Jesus faster than the lie that says, "It all depends on you." It's subtle, but this really is the mother of all lies. It comes straight from the serpent who said, "If you do this, you will be like God." It's the lie that says, "If you fast, pray, give, or do a hundred other things and continue to do them, you'll claw your way into the throne room. You'll be a self-made god." It's diabolical nonsense.

What can stop me from continuing in the faith?

Paul tells the Colossians, "God will present you holy, unblemished, and unblameable—if you continue in the faith." This sounds like conditional salvation, but it is not. You are one with the Lord, and what God has joined together, no man can separate. Paul is saying, "In God's eyes you are already holy and perfect, but you won't see it unless you believe it. You won't walk in that truth except by faith."

You may ask, "How can I believe I am holy when my life is such an unholy mess?" You can believe it because your life is hidden in Christ and *he* is holy and unblemished. You have a need for holiness—you can't get in without it—but the good news is that Jesus meets your need. By his one sacrifice, you have been made holy and perfect forever (Hebrews 10:10, 14).

I know this is a lot to swallow, particularly if you have been raised on a diet of mixture. If you have had old covenant notions of faithfulness drummed into you, it's hard not to be anxious, especially when you stumble. But Paul's letter to the Colossians, and particularly chapter 2, is a brilliant response to the fears and anxieties of the insecure believer. Let me give you some examples.

One sign that you are not continuing in the faith is that you are more conscious of your lack than you are of the Lord's supply. You may think, *I'm not holy enough, righteous enough, or fruitful enough.* Look at how Paul corrects this misperception:

> For in Christ all the fullness of the Deity lives in bodily form, and in Christ you have been brought to fullness. (Colossians 2:9–10a)

How do you continue in the faith? By recognizing that *in Christ* you lack no good thing. *In Christ* you have received every spiritual blessing there is. "*In Christ* you have been brought to fullness." The problem is not your lack but your unbelief. If you pray, "God, please make me righteous and holy," you are no longer continuing in faith. You are giving voice to unbelief and contradicting his word, which says you are complete in him.

Instead of asking Jesus to do what he's already done, why not thank him that he's done it? "Thank you, Jesus, that in you I am as righteous and holy as you are and eternally pleasing to God!"

Another sign that you are not continuing in faith is you are focused on your failings. It takes no faith to recognize your shortcomings and mistakes. But it takes faith to agree with Paul, who said this:

> In him you were also circumcised with the circumcision made without hands, by putting off the body of the sins of the flesh, by the circumcision of Christ, buried with him in baptism, in which you also were raised with him through faith in the working of God, who raised him from the dead. (Colossians 2:11–12, NKJV)

How do you continue in the faith? By reckoning yourself dead to sin and alive to Christ. You have been raised to new life through faith in a resurrecting God. Continue in that faith. Continue trusting him and stop trying to rehabilitate the sinful corpse of who you used to be.

Another sign that you are not continuing in faith is you're trying to have a bet each way when it comes to law and grace. Maybe you think, "I'm saved by grace, but the law shows me how to live." No, it doesn't. The law is not the Holy Spirit. All the law will do is point out your faults and condemn you. It shows you what you are doing wrong but does nothing to help you live right.

When Paul says, "You are free from accusation—if you continue in the faith," he's saying, "The condemning ministry of the law can't touch those who are trusting in Jesus." If your conscience is accusing and condemning you, then you're not walking in faith. You're saying, "My badness is greater than God's goodness and I am beyond his grace." That's unbelief.

"But Paul, you don't know what I did." No, you don't know what *Jesus* did. There is no sin greater than his grace.

"But every time I open my Bible I realize I've broken God's commands. I'm failing left and right." Again, stop giving your voice to the condemning ministry of the law. See the cross where God not only forgave us but also ...

> ... wiped out the handwriting of requirements that was against us, which was contrary to us. And he has taken it out of the way, having nailed it to the cross. (Colossians 2:14, NKJV)

That old arrest warrant naming and shaming you as a miserable sinner is no longer in force. On the cross, Jesus not only dealt with your sins but your accusers too. They have been disarmed and defeated.

We could continue this exercise for the rest of Colossians 2, but I hope by now you are getting the point, which is this: Continuing in faith is not an old-fashioned warning to avoid sin or keep the rules. Continuing in faith means *keep trusting Jesus*. It is resting in him and his finished work.

Now that we have some idea of what it means to continue in the faith, let's look at some other scriptures that say something similar.

What is the mother of all good sermons?

> When the congregation was dismissed, many of the Jews and devout converts to Judaism followed Paul and Barnabas, who talked with them and urged them to continue in the grace of God. (Acts 13:43)

If you are ever asked to preach and are stuck for ideas, you could do worse than pinch this six-word gem from Paul and Barnabas: *Continue in the grace of God.* It's the mother of all good sermons.

Are you working so hard that you're on the verge of burnout? You need to *continue in the grace of God.* Are you worried that you you're not doing enough for Jesus? *Continue in the grace of God.* Are you distracted by generational curses, end-times anxiety, or idle talk? *Continue in the grace of God.* Are you facing financial difficulties, sickness, or demonic oppression? *Continue in the grace of God.* Want to make something of your life? *Continue in the grace of God.*

I've been told that every sermon should have three points, so here's point one: It's grace from start to finish. There's nothing else we need and nothing else that helps. Here's point two: Grace comes to us through faith alone, so continuing in the grace of God is the same as continuing in the faith. It's the same message Paul preached to the Colossians, the Galatians, and everybody else. And here's point three: Since grace is another word for Jesus, the message is, "Keep your eyes fixed on Jesus." Whatever your problem, see Jesus as your solution.

To continue in grace is to keep trusting in Jesus. It's being unmoved from the hope held out in the gospel. It's being continually grateful for all God has done and continues to do in your life.

What will happen if I don't continue in the grace of God?

Under the old covenant, if you failed to continue you were cursed. But what is the danger in the new covenant? The danger is that you may fall from grace and lose the freedom you have in Jesus Christ. You may even come back under the condemning influence of the law.

In the passage we just looked at, Paul and Barnabas were speaking to "Jews and devout converts to Judaism" (Acts 13:43). They were addressing people who had been raised under the law. What is the greatest temptation that these former law-keepers will face? The danger is that they will do what the Galatians did and swing back to the old ways of the law. Hence Paul's exhortation:

"Continue in the grace of God. Don't go back to where you came from."

> They preached the gospel in that city and won a large number of disciples. Then they returned to Lystra, Iconium and Antioch, strengthening the disciples and encouraging them to remain true to the faith. (Acts 14:21–22a)

Different city, same message. To remain true to the faith is to continue in the faith and grace of God. It's abiding in the vine and keeping your eyes fixed on Jesus. Again, we don't continue because we fear being cursed. We remain true to the faith because it's the smart thing to do, because we'd rather be free than fettered, and because it's better to walk under grace than condemnation.

What does it mean to drift away?

> We must pay the most careful attention, therefore, to what we have heard, so that we do not drift away. For since the message spoken through angels was binding, and every violation and disobedience received its just punishment, how shall we escape if we ignore so great a salvation? (Hebrews 2:1–3a)

Here is another verse that is easy to read through an old covenant lens. Under the law, there was a real danger of tripping up simply because you weren't paying attention. The Jews went to extraordinary lengths to prevent this from happening. They discussed the law ceaselessly and made a point of teaching it to their young children. They wrote the commands on their doorframes and gates. Some even wore the law in little leather boxes attached to their hands and foreheads.[2]

Do we need to take similar steps in the new covenant? Are we in danger of drifting out of the kingdom through inattentiveness? If you are unsure of your Father's love, you may think so.

Perhaps you think the Christian walk is like walking the wrong way on those moving walkways you see at airports. You fear that if you stop moving forward you'll glide right back out of the kingdom. Or maybe you think the Christian walk is like climbing a descending escalator. It's a constant struggle, and you dare not stop lest you find yourself heading down and out of the kingdom. What an exhausting way to live.

The author of Hebrews is not saying we maintain our salvation through works and attentiveness. Instead, he's encouraging his Hebrew listeners to heed the gospel and put their faith in Jesus.

"The message spoken by angels" is a reference to the law. The Jews believed that the law had been passed down by angels (Galatians 3:19). This is why the author has just spent the previous chapter showing that Jesus is greater than the angels. He's saying, "If those who ignored the angel's message (the law) were punished, how shall we escape if we ignore the salvation revealed in this greater message (the gospel) by a greater mediator (Jesus)?"

The writer of Hebrews is saying, "Brothers, don't be like our hard-hearted forefathers who heard the gospel but didn't believe it. Jesus is greater than the angels and he is greater than Moses, so trust *him* instead of them."

The river of human life flows to the falls of eternal separation from God. However, a great Savior stands mid-stream, fishing for people and rescuing all who wish to be saved. "Pay attention," says Hebrews, "lest you glide right past him and drift away." In other words, don't miss Jesus. Don't miss grace.

If you have been rescued by Jesus, then you don't need to be rescued by Jesus, and these words of warning are not for you. If Jesus already holds you there is no chance you will drift past him. You are not safe because you are paying attention; you are safe because *he* is paying attention and no one can snatch you out of Jesus' hand (John 10:28–29).

However, if you don't know Jesus, you need to heed Hebrews 2. Don't allow the current of life carry you past the grace of God. We all need grace. Jesus has it. Take what he offers.

Why do I feel guilty and condemned?

Do you feel guilty if you miss a meeting or fail to read your Bible? Do you feel condemned for not praying, giving, or fasting enough? If so, you have to ask yourself, "Why?" Since your heavenly Father is not in the business of sending his kids on guilt trips, why do you feel guilty? Since there is no condemnation for those in Christ Jesus, why do you feel condemned?

There can be only one answer. You are not continuing in the grace and faith of God. You have allowed yourself to be distracted from Jesus. You are more conscious of your imperfections than his sublime perfections. This is not healthy.

What is the cure for guilt and condemnation? Look to the cross that divides the covenants. See Jesus, who died to set you free from the demands of the law. In him you have already passed the test. You have been granted an eternal A+ for righteousness and holiness. You will never be any more righteous and holy than the moment you became one with the Lord.

To continue in the faith is to hold fast to Jesus. It is refusing to be suckered into empty religion or conned into self-trust. It is being grounded and settled in Christ and remaining unmoved from the hope of the gospel. It is giving thanks to God who has reconciled you to himself and will present you as holy in his sight, without blemish and free from accusation.

19. What Happens to Christians Who Stray?

What happens to Christians who stray or follow another Jesus, or another gospel? This is not a hard question to answer because it happened in the Bible. The consequences of going astray are well documented. Yet the question is worth asking because many don't know the answer. Or, rather, they have the wrong answer, which is this:

> What happens when Christians stray? They fall from grace, prompting a loving God to discipline them with punishment. If they don't repent they'll lose their salvation and be eternally condemned.

The bit about falling from grace is true, but the rest is a big fat lie. Your heavenly Father's discipline never takes the form of punishment—that's old covenant thinking—and those who have been found by Jesus cannot be lost by Jesus.

Someone once said, "If you tell a lie big enough and keep repeating it, people will eventually come to believe it." The reason most Christians believe they can lose their salvation if they stray is because they have heard it over and over again. But it's not actually in the Bible. It is an extra-Biblical fabrication parroted by those who would distract you from Christ and his perfect work. It is a lie that will cause you to trust yourself and your staying power instead of standing on Jesus and the unshakeable foundation of his love and grace.

I'm sorry if this sounds harsh, but it's not nearly as harsh as telling your brothers and sisters they are in danger of hellfire. And it's not nearly as harsh as speaking guilt and condemnation over those whom Christ has justified.

"So what will happen to me if I stray from the Lord?" Well hopefully you won't stray, but if you do, you won't lose your salvation. It's just not possible. But straying or falling from grace does have consequences, as we will see. Before we look at those, let's look at the act itself.

199

How do we fall from grace?

You sometimes hear of a person falling from grace, meaning they have fallen into sin and out of favor. Typically this is said of famous Christians who have lost their ministries because of some indiscretion. But while it is possible to fall out of favor with people, you cannot sin your way out of God's favor.

God's favor is unmerited. That's why it's called grace. You can't earn it by doing good any more than you can lose it by doing bad. Where sin abounds, grace does much more abound. If you fall into sin you fall into more grace. I'm not encouraging sin. I'm saying grace is for sinners. Jesus didn't die for perfect people with perfect teeth and perfect hair. He died for real people who make mistakes. If Jesus loved you when you were dead in sins, he will always love you. Nothing can change that. Nothing can separate you from the love of God.

So how do we fall from grace?

> You who are trying to be justified by the law have been alienated from Christ; you have fallen away from grace. (Galatians 5:4)

We fall from the high place of grace and favor when we try to merit what God has freely given us. If you think you have to work before God will bless you, you have made Christ of no value. If you're striving to make yourself pleasing and acceptable to God, you have fallen from grace.

I am so glad the book of Galatians is in the Bible because we can learn a lot from other people's mistakes. The Galatians lost their liberty in Christ by allowing themselves to be enslaved to the yoke of the law. In their case the issue was circumcision, but for us it could be anything that puts a price tag on grace—church rules, confession of sins, the spiritual disciplines, whatever. I'm not against these things. I'm saying there is nothing we can do to add or improve upon Christ's perfect work. We stand by grace alone.

The Galatians had a different view. Some guys with long faces and long knives came preaching mixture and the Galatians bought it hook, line, and sinker. But does this mean the Galatians were now unsaved, under condemnation, and hell-bound? No. Falling from grace does not mean falling out of the kingdom.

What are the consequences of falling from grace?

The NIV Bible says the Galatians alienated themselves from Christ. Other translations say they became estranged, separated, severed, and cut off. These are serious words with serious implications, but they do not imply condemnation. Who cut them off? It wasn't Christ. Who did the separating? Not Jesus. As always, he remains the thoroughly faithful husband who keeps us safe while promising that no one, not even ourselves in a moment of stupidity, can snatch us out of his hands.

Paul never tells the Galatians, "You are losing your salvation." Instead, he says, "You are indulging the flesh" (Galatians 5:13). They were becoming carnal, biting and devouring one another in vicious arguments. The danger is not that God will destroy them, but that "you will be destroyed by each other" (Galatians 5:15).

Remove grace from any community and you will soon have quarrels, strife, bickering, manipulation, envy, hatred, and all the other works of the flesh that Paul lists in Galatians 5:19–21. But none of these things will send you to hell.

When Paul reminds the Galatians that "they who do such things shall not inherit the kingdom," he's saying, "Those who belong to Christ shouldn't act like those who don't." If Christians were kicked out of the kingdom every time they walked after the flesh, heaven would be empty.

What does a straying Christian look like?

Some would say that backslider is a believer who has rejected God, returned to the world, and is now drunk, pregnant, high as a kite, and living on welfare. But this picture is a fiction. I have been in the church for five decades and I can't think of one person who has done this.

Sure, I know a few who have rebelled against the unholy demands of performance-based religion. But who wouldn't? Fleeing from religious manipulation is not straying from Jesus—usually it's running *to* Jesus, albeit by a roundabout route.

If we get our examples from the Bible, then the real strays are the Galatians reverting to the law, it's the Colossians and their precious rules, and it's the loveless Ephesians working hard for the Lord. In other words, it's Christians who are walking after the flesh. Many are sincere, caring people. They want what you and I want. But the way they go about it reveals the ugliness of the flesh rather than the beauty of Jesus.

A straying Christian is any believer who is no longer walking by faith. They may be running after the pleasures of sin, but they could also be building churches, leading missionary organizations, or preaching to millions. They could be doing any number of good deeds. But if they have become distracted from Jesus, they have lost their way.

What happens if you stray from Jesus?

If you were to wander like a stray sheep, the good news is you won't get kicked out of the kingdom. Since a Christian by definition is one who has been united with Christ, the only way you can go to hell is if Christ goes—and Christ isn't going.

Jesus is the Good Shepherd who knows his sheep. He won't lose you. Nor will he come after you with a rod to break your leg, for he is compassionate and deals gently with those going astray (Hebrews 5:1–2). Nevertheless, the Bible identifies at least ten bad things that can happen to you if you get distracted, seduced, deceived, or led astray.

1. You may end up enslaved to rule-based religion (Colossians 2:20). We never call it legalism, for that would alert us to the danger. Instead, we call it "Christian responsibility" or "duty" or "doing our part." We think, *God has done his part, now it's up to me to finish what he started.*

We worry about cheap grace (there's no such thing) and invest in a little works-insurance (there's no such thing). We tell ourselves, "I gotta pray more, fast more, attend more. I gotta witness to two people this week. I gotta be a good Christian for

Jesus." This sort of thinking appeals to our religious flesh, but it's not long before ...

2. *You'll feel unworthy and unqualified (Colossians 2:18)*. The NIV Bible says, "Do not let anyone ... disqualify you." This is not a reference to salvation, since no one can disqualify those whom God qualifies (Colossians 1:12). This is about falling under the influence of frowners, finger pointers, and self-appointed judges.

The point is not that we can disqualify ourselves, but when we get distracted from Christ and his perfect work, we start to *feel* disqualified. If we compare ourselves with others who seem to be doing better, we may begin to doubt our secure position in the Lord. Although Christ makes us worthy, we *feel* unworthy. And when that happens ...

3. *Your conscience may condemn you and sabotage your faith (1 Timothy 1:18–19)*. What does it mean to shipwreck your faith? It means you allow your condemning conscience to drill a hole in your ship of faith.

Condemnation is a faith killer. Condemnation will cause you to be timid before God, making it difficult to receive from the abundance of his grace. If God says you are holy and righteous but your conscience responds, "No, I'm a miserable sinner," it will sabotage your faith. This is why Paul encourages us to hold onto faith with a clear conscience (1 Timothy 3:9). He's saying, "Be Son-focused, not sin-focused."

I sometimes meet people who are obsessed with their sins. They are living under self-imposed condemnation and they have difficulty receiving grace. The problem is not that their sins are too great for Jesus, it's that they are being cowed by their condemning consciences. This is a problem because if you have trouble receiving grace, then ...

4. *You'll miss out on all God has in store for you (2 John 1:8)*. Jesus said those who went all out for the sake of the gospel would receive back in this life 100 times what they gave up (Mark 10:29–30). Live to reveal the good news of the kingdom and you'll be rich in eternal friends—people whose lives have been blessed by your revelation of Jesus. But if you are not walking in the power of his grace, you won't achieve anything of lasting significance. This can happen if ...

5. You get bogged down in time-wasting, life-sapping discussions (1 Timothy 1:6). In his warning about those fascinated by myths and fables, Paul did not say, "Some have turned aside *unto damnation.*" He said, "Some have turned aside to *idle talk.*" In other words, they're wasting time in conversations that are going nowhere.

An excessive interest in controversy is a sure sign one has wandered from the uncontroversial gospel (1 Timothy 1:4, 6:4). It's good to ask questions, but when it comes to the big issues of life, Jesus provides emphatic answers. At some point you have to stop asking and start believing. At some point you have to say, "Okay Jesus, let's do life together." If all you do is talk, then ...

6. You'll live a life of regret (1 Timothy 6:6–10). "Godliness with contentment is great gain," said Paul. Yet many in the church don't know they are godly, and as a result they are not content. Discontentment may cause you to wander. Paul knew folk who "wandered from the faith and pierced themselves with many sorrows."

Sorrow and regret are what you get when you run after inferior pleasures like money and fame. Only Jesus satisfies the deepest longings of your soul. Until you make Jesus your resting place ...

7. You won't mature (Luke 8:14). A lot of maturity teaching is based on the idea that you need to do more of everything in order to grow. You need to pray more, give more, serve more, and so on. But growth is a natural process. Once you plant the seed of the word in the good soil of a receptive heart, you don't need to do a thing. Growth just happens (see Mark 4:27). The only thing you can do is hinder the process by choking the seed with the cares of this world or contrary teachings.

Do you desire good teaching? Do you crave good food? Then "grow in grace and the knowledge of our Lord and Savior Jesus Christ" (2 Peter 3:18). Jesus is the best teaching and he alone is the bread of life. Everything else is junk food. If you feed on anything other than the bread of life ...

8. You'll look less and less like Jesus (2 Timothy 2:16–18). Review this list and you will see nothing that describes the Lord. Was Jesus enslaved to religious demands? Did Jesus cast off his good conscience when accused of law-breaking? Did Jesus indulge time-wasters and get bogged down in idle chatter? No. Everything about Jesus speaks of life, freedom, and intentional living.

Paul said, "Those who indulge in godless chatter become more and more ungodly" (2 Timothy 2:16). In a sense, you are what you talk about because what you talk about reveals your heart. Jesus spoke about his Father because his Father is his treasure. Conversely, the Father's treasure is Jesus. It's also you and me. But if you don't know that ...

9. You'll fear God's punishment (1 John 4:17–18). Those who are secure in their Father's love can look forward to judgment day with confidence. But those who are insecure will wonder, *Have I done enough? Will God find fault with me?* These are the questions asked by those who have wandered from the faith and fallen from the secure place of God's grace. If this describes your thoughts, then ...

10. You'll be ashamed (but not condemned) when Jesus comes (1 John 2:28). John doesn't say, "Abide in Christ or you will lose your salvation." He says, "Abide in Christ so you won't feel like a fruitless schmuck when he returns," or words to that effect. This is how the Message Bible translates John's words:

> And now, children, stay with Christ. Live deeply in Christ. Then we'll be ready for him when he appears, ready to receive him with open arms, with no cause for red-faced guilt or lame excuses when he arrives. (1 John 2:28, MSG)

Imagine the shame some are going to have when Christ shows up and all their futile attempts to impress him are burned up in the splendor of his glory. All our manmade programs, all our self-efforts—*poof!*—gone in a flash of flame. How embarrassing to arrive at the wedding feast with the smell of smoke in your hair (1 Corinthians 3:15).

We have listed ten things that happen when we stray from Jesus, but we haven't yet asked the critical question, which is this:

Why do we stray?

Why did Adam eat the forbidden fruit? Why did the prodigal leave home? Why do any of us walk away from God? There is one reason and one reason only — we lose sight of our Father's love for us.

Jesus told the Ephesian Christians, "You have left your *protos agape*," or primary love (Revelation 2:4). What is our primary love? It is not our love for him; it is a revelation of his love for us. As John says again and again, love originates in God:

> Love comes from God ... This is love: not that we loved God, but that he loved us ... We love because he first loved us. (1 John 4:7a, 10, 19)

You were made to receive and respond to your Father's love. If you become distracted from your true source of love, you will wander the earth in search of it. You may search for love and affirmation through religion or worldly pleasures, but until you encounter the love of God expressed in Jesus, you will be a restless wanderer, a stray in need of a shepherd.

Why would Paul pray that we might know the love of Christ that surpasses knowledge (Ephesians 4:18–19)? Because there is a danger you might *not* know. You might forget it or leave it. God's love is like air for us. We cannot live without it. When we fall from the high place of his love, everything gets complicated. Our minds become corrupted from the simplicity that is in Christ. We start thinking, *I know God loves me, but ...*

And that's the thin edge of a bad wedge.

Next thing you know, the good news is not so good anymore. It needs qualifying. It needs balance. Those scriptures that once filled you with joy are now tempered by contrary scriptures calling for effort and toil. The Christian life, which you were told would be an adventure, proves to be hard work, a burden on top of your already exhausting life.

How do we find our way back?

Lose sight of God's love and the odds are good you will experience most of the bad things listed above. Perhaps this has already happened to you. You may be enslaved to the expectations of others or crippled with guilt and regret. Don't despair; it's not the end of the world. There is a way back.

When the Ephesians wandered from their first love, their first love came looking for them. And when he found them he showed them the way home, and here it is:

> Remember the height from which you've fallen! Repent, and do what you did at first. (Revelation 2:5a, NIV1984)

Remember! What a simple yet powerful remedy for those who have strayed. Why did the prodigal head home? He remembered the height from which he had fallen. What will bring you back when you stray into sin or dead works? Remembering the high and lofty love of your heavenly Father. His love is your true home. It's where you belong.

Jesus says, "Repent," but not in the old covenant fashion of turning from sin. Rather, it's "Repent, and do what you did at first." What did you do when you first came to Christ? Can you remember? You probably didn't do much at all other than receive his love and favor. "Do *that*," says Jesus. "Stop doing this other stuff and receive from me. Stop trying to impress me with your labor and let me impress you with my love."

It really is that simple.

Rest in the love of God and you will never put a foot wrong; but miss his love and you will miss everything. This is why the number one takeaway in the New Testament, and the number one message preached by every gospel preacher, is to abide, remain, hold fast to, and dwell in the love of God. Jesus said it best:

> I've loved you the way my Father has loved me. Make yourselves at home in my love. (John 15:9, MSG)

Make God's loving embrace your permanent resting place, and it will be impossible for anyone to lead you astray. When you allow yourself to be apprehended by the wild and relentless love of your mighty Father, no one will be able to seduce you out of it.

20. What Are Eternal Rewards?

There's an old story about a man who wanted to take his wealth to heaven. His minister said, "You can't take it with you." But the man replied, "I'm going to try." Nearing death, he sells all he has and buys two gold bars. "Bury me with my gold," he says. His plan works and he finds himself outside the gates of heaven with his precious gold. Holding up the two bars he says to St. Peter, "Look, you *can* take it with you." But St. Peter is puzzled. "You brought paving stones?!"

The joke works because it plays to our confusion regarding the riches of heaven. We know there are heavenly rewards, because Jesus says so, but what are they? Some say God is going to dispense treasure, mansions, and even cities to those who have proven faithful. "There had better be some reward for my hard work—a gold star at least—otherwise why I am working?" Others say there are no rewards at all. "Everything comes to us by grace alone, so there can be no rewards for effort."

I have problems with both views. My problem with the God-of-the-gold-stars is that he promotes a servant mentality when we are sons. And my problem with the idea that there are no rewards, is that it contradicts what Jesus said:

> Lay up for yourselves treasures in heaven, where neither moth nor rust destroys and where thieves do not break in and steal. (Matthew 6:20, NKJV)

Paul said something similar:

> The one who plants and the one who waters have one purpose, and they will each be rewarded according to their own labor. (1 Corinthians 3:8)

Rewarded according to his labor? How does that fit in the economy of grace? In the Greek the word for *reward* means pay or wages. *God is going to pay us like a paymaster?* How does that work?

The issue of eternal rewards or heavenly treasures is riddled with question marks. It's a subject that has been abused by some

("Store up treasure by giving to my ministry") and left in the too-hard basket by others. Grace-minded folk seem particularly allergic to any talk of earning rewards, and this is understandable. Grace and rewards just don't go together. And yet, here we have Jesus (Mr. Grace) and Paul (the apostle of grace) saying they do.

"You must be reading this wrong. Don't you know that in Christ we are heirs of all things? What need have we of rewards?" It's true that Jesus is our reward, and what greater reward could there be?

> No one can please God without faith, for whoever comes to God must have faith that God exists and rewards those who seek him. (Hebrews 11:6, GNB)

What is the reward of the seeker but to find that which is sought? If you are searching for God you will find him and he will be your very great reward (see Genesis 15:1). Whatever the treasures of heaven may be, they are nothing in comparison with Jesus, who is *the* reward for those who seek him. This is why those who are slaving for mansions are misguided. When Jesus is your home, what need have you of mansions?

This is not the place where I talk about our inheritance in Christ. All you need to know about that is it's good! Even if you are the newest Christian or the eleventh-hour worker, you will be as richly blessed as the oldest, most faithful saint. Eternity will not be divided into the haves and have-nots, for we are all one in Christ.

But we can distinguish Christ our reward from the heavenly treasure that Jesus said can be stored up, and the rewards Paul said are given according to our labor. At the risk of sounding like a grace-killer, let me say *all* believers have a glorious inheritance in Christ, but *some* will also get eternal rewards. There is a difference. Our inheritance comes to us through grace alone, while eternal rewards can be worked for and accumulated.

But eternal rewards may not be what you think.

What are heavenly rewards?

If there are heavenly rewards, what are they? Some say it's material wealth. "You can't take it with you, but you can send it on ahead." So the old joke about the gold bars is no joke at all. Yet if we have money in eternity, what would we spend it on? Will there be cinemas and restaurants and mini-golf? And what happens if you run out of money after a million years or so? If no one is working or playing the heavenly stock market, won't everyone end up poor in the long run?

These are silly questions because this is a silly scenario. Yet it's one I used to preach. I used to talk about lazy Christians using my heavenly lawn as a campsite. I figured I would get a mansion (I was working so hard) and they would get pup tents. What was I thinking?

Others say heavenly rewards are positions of authority. Do well down here and you'll get a city or province up there. I suppose that's fine if you want to be a mayor or governor, but it's not much of a reward if you don't. And what happens if there aren't enough cities to go around? Will Jesus say, "We ran out of places to govern so we'll make you a playground monitor"? Have fun doing that for eternity.

A big part of the problem is we're trying to picture heavenly rewards with an earthly mindset, and it just won't work. What is highly valued here may not amount to a hill of beans there. We have to see this from the Father's point of view.

What are eternal rewards? What is our heavenly treasure? The answer may surprise you, but it's people.

> Children are a heritage from the Lord, offspring a reward from him. (Psalm 127:3)

This psalm is not just talking about biological children. God has bigger plans for you and they involve spiritual children. Lots of them. Dozens. Hundreds. Thousands. Millions. Don't limit God. Just as Abraham was called to be the father of many nations, so are you.

Jesus said those who followed him would be fishers of men. What is a fisherman's reward? It's fish, or people in this case.

What is the reward of the one who sows and waters the good seed? It's a harvest of people.

What is treasure that never wears out and cannot be stolen? It's people.

God gave me this revelation at a time when Camilla and I were asking, "Do we want another child?" Having a child is the biggest decision a couple can make. You have to ask, "Is there room in our lives for another person? Can we afford the cost of raising a child?" Do you know that God is not troubled by these questions? He has plenty of room and can easily afford it.

In my heart I felt my Father say, "I want more kids! I *always* want more kids!" His heart bursts with love that craves expression. Just as a painter has to paint and a writer has to write, a father has to father. It's what he does. I'm not sure how many children I am capable of fathering, but God is a far bigger Father than me. He has no limits. His heart cries, "I treasure children. The more, the better!"

In Matthew chapter 5, Jesus introduces God as our heavenly Father. In Matthew chapter 6, Jesus says he is a Father who rewards us. What is a father's reward? It is children.

Jesus exhorts us to store up treasures in heaven. Although God is our Treasure, he is not saying, "Store up God." How would we do that? He's saying, "Be fruitful and multiply so that when this moth-eaten, money-grubbing world passes away, you will have treasures in heaven — spiritual children, and grandchildren, and great-grandchildren."[1]

I admit, this was a startling revelation. I grew up in an average-sized family and planned to have an average-sized family of my own. It never occurred to me that God isn't your average Father with average dreams. His desire is to grow the world's largest family. This is obvious once you see it, but I hadn't seen it. But someone who had was the apostle Paul.

What was Paul's reward?

Paul says we are rewarded for our labor. What labor is more rewarding than the labor of childbirth? As in the natural, so in the spiritual. What could be more fulfilling than co-laboring with the Lord to create new life? You tell someone the good news, the lights go on, a smile dawns on their face, and you realize that you and the Holy Spirit just did something special. A moment ago this person had no great regard for Jesus; now they're shining with his very life. They just became a new person, one who will learn to call God, "Abba, Father." It truly is a miracle.

The Father-heart of God beat within Paul with such intensity that he felt compelled to preach the gospel. He didn't do it for mansions or money but people.

> Though I am free and belong to no one, I have made myself a slave to everyone, to win as many as possible. (1 Corinthians 9:19)

Paul had a deep desire to raise spiritual offspring. Through the gospel he became a father to the Corinthians and a mother to the Thessalonians. He called men like Timothy and Onesimus his sons in the Lord. And when he saw those he had nurtured standing firm in Christ, he said, "Now we really live."[2]

Seeing people get zapped by grace is about the greatest thrill on earth. I've seen people healed, families restored, and addictions broken. Just yesterday I helped save a marriage simply by dispensing grace. What a buzz!

Outside of the Lord himself, there is no greater reward than co-laboring with the Holy Spirit to reproduce the life of Christ in others. Paul understood this and bragged about it:

> For what is our hope, our joy, or the crown in which we will glory in the presence of our Lord Jesus when he comes? Is it not you? Indeed, you are our glory and joy. (1 Thessalonians 2:19–20)

Perhaps you've heard it said that God keeps a photo of you in his wallet. Well, Paul kept photos of the Thessalonians in his. They were his children in the Lord, and he delighted in them just as God delights in you. They were his crown, his joy, and his eternal reward.

When Solomon said children are a reward from the Lord, he was quoting an old covenant law (see Deuteronomy 28:4). If children are a reward under the death-dealing ministry of the law, how much more should we expect offspring under life-giving grace? There's no life in the law, but grace is fertile. It is the nature of grace to reproduce good fruit among those who receive it.

What are eternal friends?

The strangest parable Jesus ever told was about a man who cheats on his boss and is then praised for doing so (see Luke 16:1–8). The parable of the shrewd manager is puzzling. What is Jesus trying to tell us? That it's okay to cook the books, diddle the figures, and engage in white-collar crime? No, Jesus isn't encouraging dishonesty. He's telling us how to plan for the future:

> And I say to you, make friends for yourselves by unrighteous mammon, that when you fail, they may receive you into an everlasting home. (Luke 16:9, NKJV)

The punchline of the parable is "make friends" — real friends you can enjoy into eternity. "When you fail" is a reference to kicking the bucket. We have an opportunity in this lifetime to make friends who will receive us in the next. How do we do that? By investing ourselves into people, showing love, and giving grace.

The problem is we're often too busy for others. Our lives are so filled with errands, exams, bills, deadlines, and meetings that we have no time for people. Relationships have been reduced to text messages and "likes" on Facebook. In these busy days, we need to hear the words of Jesus more than ever. "Be shrewd like the manager and use the resources of this world to get a return that lasts into the next."

In the story, the shrewd manager goes around writing down the debts of others. That's what we do when we tell people the good news. We're announcing the year of Jubilee and the cancellation of all debts. "God holds nothing against you. He is for you and wants you to be free from guilt and shame." We have the happy job of providing freedom to a debt-conscious world.

> Whoever can be trusted with very little can also be trusted with much ... (Luke 16:10a)

The "very little" is the unrighteous mammon; the friends we make are the "much." The wealth of this age doesn't last. Moth, rust, and thieves diminish it. But friends in Christ last forever. Friends are the only thing you can take with you.

We tend to pick friends who look like us, act like us, and think like us. But Jesus made friends with people who were nothing like him and then empowered them to become like him. He showed grace to a crooked little thief called Zacchaeus, and the man turned into a giver. He shone a light on a dark soul called Saul, and the man became a firebrand. Jesus lived and died for his friends. He even made friends out of his enemies.

Making friends is not always easy, but Jesus shows how to do it. He made time for people. He went to their parties and weddings, and generally got involved in their lives. Jesus said one good way to make friends is to have a feast:

> When you give a banquet, invite the poor, the crippled, the lame, the blind, and you will be blessed. Although they cannot repay you, you will be repaid at the resurrection of the righteous. (Luke 14:13–14)

In this world, people throw parties to socialize and network. They invite others in the hope of getting something in return. But Jesus said we can also throw parties to make eternal friends by inviting those who cannot pay us back.

How are we repaid at the resurrection of the righteous? Through friends. Do you see? Those needy folk aren't going to be needy forever. One day they will shine with glory and they will thank you for sharing your life with them.

You don't need a pulpit to proclaim the gospel of grace. You just need a table, preferably with food on it, and a little wine, or juice if you prefer. Think how often Jesus ate with people. He probably sat down and ate more often than he stood and preached. That's how Jesus made friends.

What makes the poor special?

Now that we see the best rewards are people — the friends we make and the children we raise — we begin to understand why Jesus made such a fuss over the poor. "Give to the poor, invite the poor, help the poor." It's not that God loves the poor more than the rich, it's that the poor are a better investment. They are the low-hanging fruit.

When it comes to the gospel, the poor have advantages over the rich. They haven't been numbed by the false and fleeting comforts of this world. Aware of their needs, they are ready to meet the One who promises to supply all of our needs in Christ Jesus. The table of the Lord's abundance has been laid for all, but only the hungry are grateful.[3]

Do you remember the rich young man who asked Jesus what he should do to inherit eternal life? Jesus asked him if he knew the commandments, and the man said he had kept them since he was a boy. Then Jesus looked at him, loved him, and said this:

> One thing you lack. Go, sell everything you have and give to the poor, and you will have treasure in heaven. Then come, follow me. (Mark 10:21)

There's a double whammy here. First, the young man thinks he's a good law-keeper, but Jesus knows he isn't. He's an idol-worshipper, trusting in uncertain riches. Second, he's planning for eternity, but he's going about it in the wrong way. He's investing in himself and his self-righteous performance.

Jesus loves this guy. He doesn't want him to miss out on grace. So first he gives him law so that he might recognize his need for

216

grace, and then he tells him how to make eternal friends. "Give to the poor. Throw parties for the downtrodden and the outcast." Jesus isn't just trying to get him into heaven. He wants to set him up for eternal life with lots of friends.

Giving to the poor won't make you righteous, but it may help you make eternal friends. That's not just good advice for rich young rulers, for Jesus said the same thing to his disciples:

> Sell your possessions and give to the poor. Provide purses for yourselves that will not wear out, a treasure in heaven that will never fail, where no thief comes near and no moth destroys. (Luke 12:33)

Jesus isn't calling us to a life of poverty. He's giving us practical tips on how to gather the only treasure that lasts. There is nothing wrong with owning a nice house and car. But if all you have to show for your life is a bunch of moth-eaten, rusty toys, then you have not spent wisely. You've made inferior investments and settled for an empty life when you could have a life full of friends and children.

Some think giving to the poor earns us heavenly brownie points. If that were the case, why did Jesus do it (John 13:29)? Jesus didn't need to curry favor with God. Jesus reached out to the poor because it was the smart thing to do. He did it because the needy respond to grace. Jesus preached the gospel to everyone but made a point of preaching the good news to the poor (see Matthew 11:5).

What does money have to do with this? Why does Jesus exhort us to give? We might say it's because a gift opens a door for the giver (Proverbs 18:16). But the real reason is because we care. Our heart is for people, and where your heart is there your treasure will be. If you love people, you will invest in them, not because you have to but because you want to.

We don't help the poor to buy opportunities for preaching the gospel. That's manipulation and it fools no one. We do it for love and no other reason. "If I give all I possess to the poor, but have not love, I gain nothing" (1 Corinthians 13:3). So don't put tracts on the banqueting table and don't ambush your guests with a sermon. Just love them. Spend money on them. Give them the best food you can and put flowers on the table. Imagine Jesus was coming for dinner and prepare accordingly.

"But Paul, how will our guests hear the gospel if we don't tell them?" You have to trust God. Don't try and make things happen. Just follow the Holy Spirit and go with the flow. You may get an opportunity to talk about Jesus or heal the sick, or you may not. But have no agenda other than the goal of loving without any expectation of getting something in return. Unconditional love is a rare commodity in this world. It speaks louder than any sermon and points to the grace of a good God.

Jesus preached the gospel *and* gave to the poor. Paul did the same. Like Jesus, he understood the significance of the poor and was enthusiastic about giving to them:

> All they asked was that we should continue to remember the poor, the very thing I had been eager to do all along. (Galatians 2:10)

Paul didn't give to the poor out of religious duty or to please the law-conscious. He did it because he loved people and wanted to win as many as possible. He understood that grace goes furthest where it's most needed. He knew that Jesus came especially for the sick and the sinful and that the kingdom of God is for the poor.[4]

At the start of this book I asked, "Who's your Daddy?" Here at the end, it's fitting that I ask, "Who are your children?" One question follows the other. The more you know your Father's heart, the more you want to be a father or mother yourself. That's how love works. We receive it, get changed by it, then give it away.

Perhaps the story of your life has been one of barrenness and fruitlessness. Perhaps you have tried to preach the gospel and little came of it. Can I suggest you stop trying and start resting in the love of your Father? There is no pressure here. Your place in the kingdom is as secure as Jesus, and in him you are already the heir of all things. You have nothing to prove. This isn't about putting you to work but putting *grace* to work. How do you do that? I can't tell you. What works for me won't work for you. But the Holy Spirit isn't short of ideas. Stay focused on Jesus and he will lead you on a grace adventure tailor-made for you.

You may be thinking, "I've got to start hosting banquets. I've got to get some eternal friends." But if you don't have the gift for hospitality, you'll be a lousy host. You may never host a banquet. You might do something completely original that no one has ever thought of before. Don't limit your Father. He made you, he knows you, and he's got some ideas about how you can do this. Ask him to show you. And then brace yourself because I guarantee you God's ideas are bigger and better than anything you could come up with on your own.

The gospel of grace is good news for the barren, for it frees us from the pressure to produce and empowers us to do that which we could never have done alone. Grace makes us abundantly fruitful.

Manmade religion says you have to perform and make it happen, but grace simply says, "Trust Jesus and allow him to express his life through you." Religion will make you cry in fruitless frustration, but grace makes you sing and dance for joy!

Notes

Preface: Ask and you shall receive
1. You may ask, "Will there be a study guide or discussion guide to go with this book?" *The Gospel in Twenty Questions* is eminently suited to small-group discussion, but as for a study guide, there won't be one. I'm not a fan of them. Instead, I recommend a discussion strategy I learned from Wayne Jacobsen. Get everyone in your group to read the same chapter, then, when you meet, ask two questions: (1) What did you like about this chapter? (2) What ticked you off? Good discussion is sure to follow.

Chapter 1. Who's your Daddy?
1. See James 1:17, 1 John 3:1, and the opening verses of most of Paul's letters.
2. See John 5:17-20, 8:28, 12:49-50. In the four gospels, Jesus mentions the kingdom 106 times and God the Father about 175 times. However, it would be incorrect to think Jesus treated his Father as merely one subject among many. His Father was the lens through which Jesus made sense of everything. For instance, when discussing the kingdom, he described it as "my Father's kingdom" (Matthew 26:29).
3. A.W. Tozer, *The Knowledge of the Holy.* HarperCollins: New York, 1961, p.1.
4. See Isaiah 6:1-2, Ezekiel 1:26-28, Daniel 7:9-10.

Chapter 2. What really happened at the cross?
1. Pierre Morel (director). *Taken.* 2008. EuropaCorp: France.
2. Paul describes us as slaves in Romans 6:17, 20 and Galatians 4:8. Throughout Romans, Paul describes sin as a personality with desires and an agenda. If you're open to his metaphor, we might as well go the whole way and say sin is another name for the devil. Consider the evidence. Both sin and Satan seek to devour us (Genesis 4:7, 1 Peter 5:8) and kill us (Romans 7:11, John 8:44). Neither could touch Jesus (Hebrews 4:15, John 14:30), and both have been defeated by him (Hebrews 9:26, John 12:31). At the end of the story the devil is thrown into the lake of fire (Revelation 20:10) and so is death, which is the fruit of sin (Revelation 20:14).
3. Andy Wachowski and Laurence Wachowski (directors). *The Matrix.* 1999. Warner Bros: USA.
4. See Ephesians 4:18, Titus 3:3, and Hebrews 2:15.
5. In Biblical times certain individuals were regarded as blameless and without sin. For instance, the Bible records that Jesus' Uncle Zechariah and Aunt Elizabeth observed "all the Lord's commands and decrees blamelessly" (Luke 1:6). Since the law brings knowledge of sin, we might conclude they were sinless. They were do-gooders of the highest order. Yet God is not impressed by good behavior, but faith, and they were faithless — at least Zechariah was. When the angel Gabriel brought him news that his prayers had been answered and Elizabeth would soon have a son, Zechariah responded with doubt and incredulity. "Do you expect me to believe this? I'm an old man and my wife is an old woman" (Luke 1:18, MSG). The angel had brought good news but was

met with unbelief. He responded by silencing Zechariah's unbelieving mouth until the promise was fulfilled.

6. The condemnation of a furious God is no small thing. The word *condemned* in Romans 8:3 is the same word Peter uses to describe what God did to Sodom and Gomorrah (2 Peter 2:6). God's condemnation should never scare you but give you confidence and peace. Every child needs to know their daddy is dangerous towards those who attack his family.

Chapter 3: What about the resurrection?

1. Barbara Richmond, *Jewish Insights into the New Testament,* For Your Glory: Merritt Island, FL, 1996, chapter 7.
2. C.S. Lewis, *Mere Christianity,* Collins: London, 1952, pp.52-53.
3. See Matthew 28:17. I have a hunch that Saul the Pharisee was such a person. I suspect the risen Lord tried to get his attention on several occasions, most notably when Stephen died. But Saul was a doubter. His religion blinded him to the grace of God. Jesus had to knock Saul on his seat before he started paying attention.
4. Bob George (1989), *Classic Christianity,* Harvest House: Eugene, OR, p.43.

Chapter 4: By which gospel are you saved?

1. See Ephesians 1:13 and 6:15, 1 Timothy 1:11, and Revelation 14:6. Paul tells the Romans about "my gospel" twice (Romans 2:16, 16:25) and reminds the Corinthians of the gospel "I preached" in 1 Corinthians 15:1.
2. G3344 (*metastrepho*), Thayer's Greek Lexicon, website: concordances.org/greek/3344.htm

Chapter 5: Am I under law?

1. Watchman Nee, *The Normal Christian Life,* Tyndale House: Wheaton, IL, 1957/1977, p.157.
2. See Romans 6:6, 7:17, 20. The "body of sin" in Romans 6:6 is our physical body, the place where sin is experienced. Similarly, the "body of death" in Romans 7:24 is the place where death is experienced — in our bodies. Paul is not saying our bodies are sinful for elsewhere he exhorts us to present our bodies as living and holy sacrifices to God (Romans 12:1). Don't look at your body as though it is the devil's tool. It is the temple of the Holy Spirit (1 Corinthians 6:19).
3. Some translations of Galatians 3:24 say the law is our school master or tutor. This can convey the erroneous impression that the law is our teacher. Paul is not saying this at all. The word he uses is *paidagōgos*, which describes a guardian or guide. In defining this word, Vines, in his *Expository Dictionary of New Testament Words*, notes that, "The idea of instruction is absent" (bit.ly/1eQfyxH). The law is not a teacher but a guide who leads us to the real Teacher, who is Jesus. Paul continues, "Now that faith has come, we are no longer under the supervision of the *paidagōgos*" (Galatians 3:25). If you have put your trust in Jesus, you no longer need the guidance of the law.
4. If you listen (Exodus 23:22), if you seek (Deuteronomy 4:29), if you follow (Leviticus 26:3), if you obey (Deuteronomy 28:1), if you bring (Leviticus 2:4), and if you make (Deuteronomy 23:21).

Chapter 6: How can I read the Bible without getting confused?

1. Here are the passages where James talks about the rich and powerful who infiltrate our meetings (James 2:2), exploit their workers (James 5:4), murder the innocent (James 5:6), trust in money instead of God (James 5:3), and slander the name of Jesus (James 2:7).
2. If this is news to you, you may want to read *The Gospel in Ten Words*. In chapter 2 of that book, I show how the cross radically altered the way Jesus spoke about forgiveness.
3. You may be wondering why I quote extensively from the NIV, NKJV, and the Message Bible in this book. The reason is that these are the translations preferred by Escape to Reality readers. I know this because I polled them. If they read different translations, I would quote different translations. You've got to know your audience.

Chapter 8: Am I lukewarm?

1. Why do I say we get everything besides? Because in Christ we are joint-heirs with the One who is the heir of all things (Romans 8:17, Hebrews 1:2).

Chapter 9: How do I endure to the end?

1. It's a rule with exceptions. As I write this I am thinking of David Wilkerson who, when confronted with the switchblades of Nicky Cruz and his gang, didn't run but stood and said, "You could cut me into a thousand pieces and lay them in the street, and every piece will still love you." As a result of Wilkerson's brave witness, Cruz and many gang members abandoned their violent ways and came to Jesus. How do we know when we should stay in spite of opposition? We need to hear from God. A specific word from the Lord trumps any general principle on enduring and staying safe. As he records in his 1962 book *The Cross and the Switchblade*, Wilkerson felt specifically called to the gangs of New York City. Similarly, Paul was called to remain in Corinth, a city where he faced opposition from abusive Jews. Paul may have thought about leaving—he'd done it before. But in a vision, the Lord told him, "Don't be afraid, keep speaking, no one will harm you." So Paul stayed another 18 months and established a famous church (see Acts 18:1–11).
2. See Matthew 12:14–15, Luke 4:28–30, John 10:31–39, 11:53–54.
3. Philip Yancey, *What's So Amazing About Grace?* OMF Literature: Manila, 1997, p.64.

Chapter 10: Who can take communion?

1. Jesus took the bread and "gave thanks" or *eucharisteō* (Luke 22:19).
2. G1381 (*dokimazō*), Strong's Exhaustive Concordance, website: concordances.org/greek/1381.htm

Chapter 11: How does God deal with us when we sin?

1. To their credit, the translators who prepared the 2011 version of the NIV removed the word *guilt* from John 16:8. In the latest edition of the NIV, this passage now reads, "When he comes, he will prove the world to be in the wrong about sin and righteousness and judgment." However, the word guilt remains in the New International Readers' Version.

2. The Greek word for *convict* is *elegchō* (G1651) which can be translated as *admonish, convince, reprove*. But in his *Expository Dictionary of New Testament Words*, Vines notes, "the real meaning here is exposed" (http://bit.ly/1awcOFC). This interpretation fits with scripture. "Have nothing to do with the fruitless deeds of darkness, but rather expose (*elegchō*) them ... Everything exposed (*elegchō*) by the light becomes visible" (Ephesians 5:11, 13). The Holy Spirit is in the business of turning on the lights and revealing the truth. A classic example would be Saul on the road to Damascus.
3. *Epanorthōsis* (1882), Strong's Exhaustive Concordance, website: concordances.org/greek/1882.htm

Chapter 13: Is it God's will for me to be sick?
1. G4982 (*sozo*), Strong's Exhaustive Concordance, website: concordances.org/greek/4982.htm
2. Live under the law and your health will suffer. Is it any coincidence that people were long-lived before Mt. Sinai but after the law was given began to die younger?
3. In a literal translation, this passage speaks of "being judged by the Lord." This is a reference to the witness of the Holy Spirit who will constantly seek to affirm that we are the righteousness of God in Christ Jesus. In Christ, we have been judged and thoroughly approved.

Chapter 15: What is the unforgivable sin?
1. This isn't to say the whole world is saved, for we all need to respond to the grace of God by faith (Ephesians 2:8). Everyone is forgiven, but not everyone has received the gift of his righteousness (Romans 1:17).
2. I would love to take credit for this little gem about God sinning by harboring unforgiveness, but I stole it (with permission) from my friend Cornel Marais. He wrote about it here: http://bit.ly/13n0saV
3. G988 (*blasphēmia*) Thayer's and Smith's Bible Dictionary, website: www.biblestudytools.com/lexicons/greek/kjv/blasphemia.html

Chapter 16: Once saved, always saved?
1. G728 (*arrabón*), Strong's Exhaustive Concordance, website: http://bibleapps.com/greek/728.htm
2. There are more than 200 scriptures in the New Testament that touch on the believer's security. Space precludes me from looking at them all in this book. However, you can find additional commentary at EscapeToReality.org on a page entitled "Eternal Security."

Chapter 17: Is the Christian race a marathon?
1. Dean Karnazes, "Badwater blues: Why does every year seem tougher than the last," Badwater.com, website: http://bit.ly/1aTkBKc, accessed 3 November 2013.
2. Acts 20:24, 1 Corinthians 9:24, Hebrews 12:1, 2 Timothy 4:7.
3. The first promise comes from 1 Corinthians 1:8-9. The second comes from 2 Corinthians 1:21-22.

4. Paul says elsewhere, "May I never boast except in the cross of our Lord Jesus Christ, through which the world has been crucified to me, and I to the world" (Galatians 6:14). The believer shares Paul's boast; the unbeliever does not.

Chapter 18: What does it mean to continue in the faith?
1. The story of Achan and his troubles is found in Joshua 7. The story of Uzzah is in 2 Samuel 6.
2. Sources: Exodus 13:1–16, Deuteronomy 6:6–9, 11:18–21. The little law-holding boxes are called phylacteries. Jesus criticized the Pharisees for wearing ostentatious phylacteries (Matthew 23:5).

Chapter 20: What are eternal rewards?
1. This idea of viewing people treasure is an old one (see Deuteronomy 7:6, 14:2, 26:18). In God's eyes, people are treasure.
2. Paul reminded the Corinthians, "I became your father through the gospel" (1 Corinthians 4:15). He told the Thessalonians, "We were gentle among you, like a mother caring for her little children" (1Thessalonians 2:7, NIV1984). And like a parent, he was thrilled when he saw them standing firm in the Lord (1 Thessalonians 3:8).
3. I am making some sweeping generalizations here. Being poor is no guarantee that you will be aware of your need for grace just as being rich doesn't mean you will be ignorant. But you are more likely to encounter the poor *in spirit* among the needy and downtrodden than those who think they've got it made (see Luke 6:24).
4. Jesus said the poor are blessed because theirs is the kingdom of God (Luke 6:20). In truth, the kingdom is for everyone, but only those who know they are poor and needy are running in. Those rich in self-righteousness don't see their need for grace.

Scripture Index

Acknowledgements

I am grateful to the many individuals who assisted in the writing of this book. Some of the material here was based on posts published on Escape to Reality. I am thankful for the many hundreds of E2R readers who took the time to comment on these posts. Their feedback helped me clarify my thinking and sharpen my writing.

Each chapter in this book was read by several people prior to publication. I want to thank Steve Barker, Jennie Lawson, Cornel Marais, Steve Hackman, Tammy Hackman, Brandon Petrowski, and Peter Wilson for their constructive feedback and encouragement on these early drafts. I am also grateful to three sharp-eyed proofreaders; Camille Lee, Judy Fake, and Kirsty Chaignon.

As always, my biggest thanks goes to my wife Camilla. Without her loving support and incredible grace, this book would not have seen the light of day.

Escape to Reality

If you still have questions about the gospel of grace, you can find answers at Paul Ellis's website. Visit EscapeToReality.org and you will discover:

- an archive of almost 400 grace-based articles
- reviews of more than 40 grace books
- resources for your private study or small group
- real stories of lives radically changed by grace

The good news may be the best news you never heard!

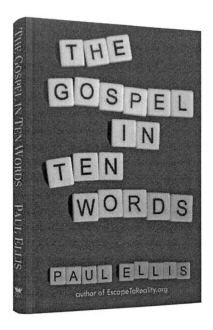

At a time when many are hearing mixed messages about the love of God, *The Gospel in Ten Words* is a welcome reminder of the good news revealed by Jesus.

This book will take you to the heavenly treasure rooms of grace and leave you awestruck at the stunning goodness of God.

You will discover the secret to walking in divine favor and experiencing freedom in every aspect of your life.

You will learn who you really are and why you were born.

Best of all, you will come face to face with the One who has called you to the thrilling adventure of living loved.

AVAILABLE NOW!